Locked On Leadership

THE TACTICAL BUSINESS GUIDE
TO CREATING A CULTURE
OF COURAGE, CARING
AND CONSISTENCY

Contents

Introduction

*"The most vital quality a soldier can
possess is self-confidence."*

~ GEN. GEORGE S. PATTON, JR.

t's the early 1990's, and I am the Radar Intercept Officer (RIO)
in the wing aircraft of (2) F-14 Tomcats. We're tasked with protecting a strike group. Our mission is to fly into the target area
ahead of the bombers. We want to make sure there is no one
loitering around that might want to ruin their day.

We are high over the desert, flying in High Trail formation,
something not used since the Korean War. My F-14 Tomcat is
about 1/2 mile behind and 1,500 feet above the lead aircraft. Our
job is to make sure no one sneaks up on them from behind (we
refer to this as clearing the lead's six). Of course, our six is vulnerable because no one is behind us to watch it. This is a departure
from our standard procedure of flying combat spread, where we
are abeam of the lead aircraft and can clear each other's six, providing mutual support.

We are in this antiquated formation because two hours earlier,
during the mission brief, the pilot of the lead aircraft, our brand-
new Executive Officer (XO), changed our procedure. In the Navy,

the XO is the #2 ranked officer in the squadron, kind of like an Executive VP. The other aircrew and I argued strenuously against this change. We knew that it would put the mission and us at risk, but as the senior ranking officer in the mission, his word was final.

So here we are, high over the desert in this outdated formation when we get a radio call from the E2C Hawkeye, *"2 Bandits, 170, Angels 4, 50 miles."* With that short sentence, we know we have two confirmed bad guys, 50 miles south of us, 4,000 feet above sea level, which in this part of the world means very close to the ground.

As we pointed our aircrafts south, the lead RIO and I started looking for the bandits with our radars. We are flying towards the bandits at a relative speed of 1,000 mph. We only have about 90 seconds before we are in missile range and three minutes before we are on top of each other.

The good news is we are flying the F-14 Tomcat with the most powerful air-to-air radar system built. The bad news, we are pointing this powerful radar at the largest target around, mother earth herself, and the ground reflection effectively hides the bandits.

I start to tweak the radar, trying to filter out the ground clutter without desensitizing the receiver so much that we don't see the bandits. Meanwhile, our controller counts down the miles, 40 miles, 30 miles, no joy. All I see on my radar are ghost returns that keep disappearing. Most are false, but any of them could be the bandits. I continue to tweak. Twenty miles, 10 miles, now the hairs on the back of my neck are standing on end. We are within missile engagement range and still no radar contact.

Then, I hear the words I never wanted to without a good radar lock, *"Merge!"* This means that on our controller's radar, our images and the bandits' have merged into one and they could not tell the good guys from the bad.

My pilot, call sign "Crunch," is scanning ahead of us to make sure they don't sneak up on our lead. I immediately start looking over my shoulder—literally. Having failed to acquire them on radar and with no one watching our six, my job is to pick them up visually. Suddenly I spot two enemy fighters maneuvering towards a firing solution on our left side. I call on the radio, *"Break Left, Break Left, bandits 7 o'clock low."* The pilots react immediately and we make a hard, high G turn. My body suddenly weighs six times its normal weight. We are trying to get them to overshoot so we can reverse and hopefully maneuver into an advantageous position. Unfortunately, these pilots are good, and we quickly find ourselves out of speed and out of options. The bad guys continue to maneuver into a firing solution. It is only a matter of time. We do the only thing any self-respecting naval aviator can do when placed in a desperate position—we die an inglorious death.

Fortunately, this is a training mission. We hear *"Good Kill, return to base"* on the radio, tuck our tails between our legs and head back to base to debrief. A little demoralized and dejected, we land. Our squadron has a history and reputation for being the best in the Navy and we had our tails handed to us so fast we didn't have time to blink. As Crunch and I walk into the Ready Room, the XO looks at us and says, "Well, that didn't work out too well. I guess that's the last time I'll tell you guys how to fly a mission." Of course, we didn't believe him. Nothing in our experience had prepared us for a senior officer ceding any part of their authority to their junior officers.

This was the XO's first tactical mission with us. He had no experience with us nor knowledge of our capabilities, but he still took control and failed. He changed the way we operate, didn't listen to any of our input, and we failed gloriously. We were dubious, at best, about the future of our squadron and how life would be under the new XO. He had lost our trust—at least temporarily. However, by admitting his mistake and making himself vulnerable he planted the seed for renewed trust. Additionally, his act of contrition showed us respect. We all knew he overrode our concerns. He could have blamed us, but he didn't. He respected us enough not to deflect blame away from himself, an act that would have further eroded our trust in him. Trust and respect for your team are just some of the attributes of a locked on leader.

Since leaving the Navy, I have worked with hundreds of companies and witnessed the same story repeated—without the redemption part. Often, it's a manager or owner that hasn't worked in the field in some time who tells the employees that do the job every day how to do it. Time and time again, it has the same debilitating effect on morale and ultimately production, performance, and profits.

This is a book about leadership tactics, the day-to-day behaviors that leaders need to employ to inspire their team to achieve greatness. These tactics work in any environment, with any team, but for the purposes of this book we talk about these tactics in business settings. It doesn't matter if you are leading a newly formed team or an existing team. It doesn't matter what you did yesterday. By consistently employing these tactics, you and your team will thrive, experience improved performance, increased productivity, higher profits, and more recognition for your accomplishments—the litmus test for good leadership. I can't and don't cover every possible leadership tactic in this book, I'm not omniscient. What I do provide you are the essential leadership tactics and the strategy necessary to create your own tactics.

In Part I, I'll define a locked on leader and the essential, personal qualities you need to become one. In Part II, you'll discover the strategy to creating a high-performing team. In Part III, you'll learn how to ensure each and every member of your team has the opportunity to become high-functioning and self-sufficient. Finally, in Part IV, we'll explore specific tactics and behaviors for high-performance transformation. You'll discover how to create a culture where your team has pride in their work and enjoy themselves while being highly productive.

PART I

Essential Qualities of a Leader

"The most important thing I learned is that soldiers watch what their leaders do. You can give them classes and lecture them forever, but it is your personal example they will follow."

~ GENERAL COLIN POWELL

The most challenging part of flying fighters was not shooting down the bad guys; it was knowing which bad guys to shoot down. In a complex battlespace, your radar is inundated with returns. Unidentified radar returns are referred to as *bogeys*. Some of them are ghost images, fake returns, like I experienced during the training mission over the desert. Others are friendly aircraft on their own missions, others still may be neutral aircraft without either the knowledge or sense to stay out of contested airspace. Then there are the actual bad guys, referred to as *"bandits."* However, even bandits aren't always targets. Some are more important than others. Even the highest threats to our mission are prioritized based on specific criteria. We refer to the act of prioritization as *sorting.*

The job of the Mission Commander is to inform the rest of the flight the sorting priority. For example, he may state, "azimuth sort" meaning to sort left to right based on your position in the formation. Sequentially, each aircraft responds confirming their assigned target. Once sorted, each aircraft reports "locked" indicating they have achieved a radar lock. This meant their radar entered single target track and all the radar energy was focused on their assigned target. Each aircraft was blind to anything but their target. We would then prosecute our target until the threat no longer existed.

Leaders are inundated daily with problems. Like bogeys, the importance of these problems must be determined and prioritized. Leaders have to sort the problems, then "lock on to them" and prosecute them until they are resolved. Those who successfully do this are "Locked On Leaders." These leaders are effective and efficient. They make it look easy. This book provides you with the tools necessary to be locked on, to focus on the high threat bandits in your organization and prosecute them until they are no longer a concern.

Locked on leaders have certain personality characteristics. I am not talking about authority as there are plenty of people with authority that are not leaders and even more leaders that have no authority. There are three characteristics that are essential if you want to be an effective leader: integrity, courage, and caring. None of these qualities can be taught nor practiced intermittently. The good news is, unlike physical prowess, coordination, or natural athleticism, you don't need to be born with these traits. All you need to do is to make the decision to demonstrate them on a daily basis.

CHAPTER 1

The Consistency
of Integrity

The supreme quality for leadership is unquestionably integrity.
Without it, no real success is possible,
no matter whether it is on a section gang,
a football field, in an army, or in an office.

~ DWIGHT D. EISENHOWER

A popular meme says, "Integrity is doing the right thing, even when no one is looking." Although it catches the essence of integrity, it doesn't truly explain it. Integrity is from the Latin integritātem, which means *whole*, as in complete. If a structure is said to have integrity, it is sound or whole, undamaged. When it comes to our character, the same holds true.

We all have a unique set of beliefs, things we hold to be true. Subconsciously we prioritize these beliefs based on our personal experiences; that is, we place a value on these beliefs. This is what is meant when we talk about someone's values. The beliefs that we value the most inform our moral code, the way we make decisions about right and wrong. Our beliefs, values, and morals make up our character. When we claim to have a set of values and a moral code that is in conflict with our actual values and moral code our character is flawed and we lack integrity. You are true to yourself when you have integrity.

Of the three essential qualities of leadership, integrity is the most important. Without integrity, nothing else matters.

Enron and Integrity

Acting without integrity is a house of cards in a gale. Case in point, Enron, a Houston-based energy company. In August of 2000, Enron's stock price reached a high of $90 per share.[1] October of that year, Enron announces $638M in 3rd quarter losses and a $1.2B reduction in shareholder equity, the SEC opens up an investigation. By the end of November, the value of Enron shares plummeted to less than $1. Enron files for bankruptcy in December. When the dust settled, 16 people and one company, Arthur Andersen, Enron's auditor, were convicted of criminal acts surrounding the demise of Enron. All of this was a result of irregular accounting practices and the illegal cover-up by Arthur Anderson, all in an attempt to manipulate stock prices.

According to Enron's annual report in 2000, their core values were:

Communication - We have an obligation to communicate. Here, we take the time to talk with one another... and to listen. We believe that information is meant to move and that information moves people.

Respect - We treat others as we would like to be treated ourselves. We do not tolerate abusive or disrespectful treatment.

Integrity - We work with customers and prospects openly, honestly, and sincerely. When we say we will do something, we will do it; when we say we cannot or will not do something, then we won't do it.

Excellence - We are satisfied with nothing less than the very best in everything we do. We will continue to raise the bar for everyone. The great fun here will be for all of us to discover just how good we can really be.

Clearly, the market reacted poorly when Enron top executives, Ken Lay and Jeffrey Skilling, completely ignored Enron's core values. In the end, Lay was found guilty of six counts of security and wire fraud and was subject to a possible 45 years in prison. He died before sentencing. Jeffrey Skilling was sentenced to 24 years and 4 months from his conviction on 19 counts of securities and wire fraud.[2]

What about Arthur Andersen, the company that was responsible for auditing Enron's books? Their fraud conviction meant the SEC could not accept audits from them anymore. Arthur Andersen also cited *integrity* as a core value, but they failed to uphold integrity when they allowed one of their employees to put personal profits over Arthur Andersen values. As a result, 85,000 employees lost their jobs.

High-performing teams need consistency in leadership or they will fall into the same trap as Enron and Arthur Andersen. They need to trust that what you say, you mean. As a child, I recall hearing someone say, "Your honor is the one thing that no one can take away from you, but once you give it away, you can never get it back in its entirety." The requirement for the consistency of integrity can be onerous. We must be consistent in our words and actions. Our team must know with certainty that we say what we mean and we mean what we say. This is not always easy. The universe has a way of periodically testing our integrity.

Situations will arise where your personal interests conflict with your stated values.

When Personal Interests Clash with Values

In 2003, I started my second business, a telecommunications company selling and installing business telephone systems. To compete with bigger, better-established companies, I offered a 30-day unconditional guarantee. If you weren't happy, for any or no reason, I would take back the system and refund your money. Over the ensuing years, our excellent service reputation grew. Although I no longer needed the guarantee to attract customers, I kept it as it helped ensure that my team would always work hard to make the customer happy. Some years later, I sold two systems to a company owned by a married couple, one for their office and one for the owner's home. The husband was their chief salesman and worked from home. Apparently, he was difficult to work with. His wife, who ran the business as President, wanted to keep him away from the office.

We were replacing an existing system at their home and connecting it with the office system so it worked as one system. Unfortunately, the husband did not deal well with change. Although the new system offered many advantages over the old, it required him to learn a new way to do everything and he was unwilling to put in the effort. As we approached the 30-day mark, it became clear to me that we were never going to make him happy and that this had the potential to become a nightmare. The problem was, with all the time we spent trying to make him happy, if we pulled the system and replaced it with the old one, we would end up losing money and that would be bad for the company. A seeming dilemma, I could have said nothing, let the 30 days pass, had a profitable account and an unhappy client, or I could remind the owners of the guarantee and suggest we put the old system back in the house so the husband would be happy, lose thousands of dollars, and honor our values by prioritizing customer service, one of our stated values. Like many small businesses, cash flow was tight and that option would put a strain on the business.

The decision was easy. We knew our priority was customer satisfaction so I made the suggestion. The customer agreed, and we provided a refund to the client. We put things back and they were elated, so much so that they became one of our biggest fans. Although I didn't know this would happen when we made the decision to offer to remove the system, our financial loss was more than made up for when I shared the story with other potential customers. As a result, they saw that our promises were not just words. In addition, we received many referrals from that customer. This illustrates a truism in life, one that was stated by my last skipper who started as the XO who led the disastrous training mission. His name is George Luechauer, call sign "Luke." Luke was fond of saying, "Do right things and things happen right." I now know this means that the universe will reward good decisions. However, in order to make good decisions and maintain integrity, it takes courage.

CHAPTER 2

Courage:
the Key to Integrity

"Courage is the most important of all the virtues because without courage, you can't practice any other virtue consistently."

~ MAYA ANGELOU

The Credo Challenge and Tylenol

In 1982, James Burke was CEO and Chairman of the Board for Johnson & Johnson (J&J). At that time, Tylenol had a 35% market share, holding the high ground for over-the-counter pain relief. The next four over-the-counter pain medications didn't have the combined market share of Tylenol. In addition, Tylenol was responsible for 19% of J&J's profits.

On September 30, 1982, five people in the Chicago area died taking Tylenol laced with potassium cyanide. A day later, a sixth person died. Although the investigation quickly determined that the bottles of Tylenol had been tampered with and all incidents were limited to the Chicagoland area, J&J did something unprecedented. On October 1, James Burke announced J&J had stopped all production of Tylenol until they could assure their customer's safety. At the time, pundits predicted this to be a mortal blow to J&J. When asked if this was a difficult decision, Burke replied that it was not.

The reason this was an easy decision was their Credo spelled out their core values. This Credo has been around since 1943. In 1975, the year before Burke became the CEO, he instituted, "the Credo Challenge," a retreat where J&J management discussed if the Credo was still relevant. The first two sentences of the Credo read:

"We believe our first responsibility is to the doctors, nurses, and patients, to mothers and fathers and all others who use our products and services. In meeting their needs everything we do must be of high quality."

The fact that this is the opening paragraph makes it is clear that Johnson & Johnson values their responsibility to their patients and caregivers above all else. Because of this annual, rigorous scrutiny of the values embodied in the Credo, it was easy for James Burke to pull Tylenol off the shelves. Although they were not responsible for poisoning anyone, their packaging made it possible. When Tylenol returned to the shelf in December of that year, it was in new tamper-resistant packaging. About a year later, Tylenol regained all of its market share.

Demonstrating integrity, Burke upheld the Credo and pulled Tylenol off the market. It took courage to face down all the shareholders who saw their investments going down the drain. Through his actions, Burke demonstrated he cared deeply for his company, his customers, and his fellow man—traits of a true locked on leader.

The Tylenol poisoning was a test of Burke's integrity. At some point, your integrity will also be tested, that's a given. No doubt everyone can think of times past when you have been tested. The test to our integrity is not like a test in school where once we pass it, we never have to deal with it again. Life's tests repeat themselves time and time again. In my experience, the test of integrity is always simple in form. A situation will arise where it appears that the only way to uphold one of your self-professed values comes with a personal cost. For Burke, the potential loss was huge as 19% of their profits came from Tylenol. This could have been the death knell of the company. However, this perceived loss is a trap, an ambush, and like most ambushes, it will spring up at the last minute. For founder, CEO and Chairman of Enron, Kenneth Lay, the ambush was swift and deadly. Within three months, Enron's stock tumbled as they went from the darling of the energy sector to bankrupt.

When caught in an ambush, our military is trained to attack out if possible. They put massive firepower on a point in the ambush and attempt to break out. Burke did this when he elected to pull Tylenol off the market. This takes courage.

The problem is that ambushes are sudden, and if you don't think about the situation ahead of time, you may not react or react well. The most dangerous ambushes don't come in tactically perfect high-walled canyons with one exit. The reason is the site is so obvious that any competent military commander will take precautions to minimize the risk. The real danger is when the ambush site is well concealed, and the tactical layout is more subtle and difficult to detect. The same is true when it comes to the test of integrity.

Throughout human history, we have used stories to highlight both the virtues of those we admired as well as cautionary tales for what happens when we fail to maintain our integrity. Stories, like the Tylenol poisoning and the Enron collapse, are powerful reminders of why our values are important. Use your own stories to serve you and your team in times of doubt. The following exercise is designed to help you plan for the integrity tests to come. If you are a manager unclear about your company's values, ask. If your company doesn't have any stated values, loan the owner(s) this book or give it to them as a gift. If you are the owner or a board member and unclear about your company's true values, save this exercise until you complete the Locked On Values Exercise in Chapter 4.

LOCKED ON AMBUSH
AVOIDANCE EXERCISE

1. Review your company values one at a time.
2. For each company value, brainstorm how the value might be turned against you. In other words, what circumstances might arise where upholding this value may appear to come at a high cost?
3. Map out why the conflict you perceive is an illusion.
   a. List specifically how you will benefit from maintaining your company's integrity.
   b. List what you will lose should you fail to maintain your company's integrity.

Note: Items 3a & 3b will help you understand why it is important to maintain your integrity and what you have to lose in the long run if you don't.

4. Identify stories from your past where you maintained your integrity and how you ultimately benefited.
5. Identify times when you failed to maintain your integrity and what it ultimately cost you.
6. Memorialize the stories and make sure your team hears them often. Like The Boy Who Cried Wolf everyone should be aware of the perils of not upholding your values.

Remember, it is impossible to be an effective leader without integrity, and it is equally impossible to have a high-functioning team without an effective leader.

It takes courage to be consistent and maintain your integrity, but where will you find the courage to do it?

CHAPTER 3

Caring: How to Find Your Courage

"Being deeply loved by someone gives you strength,
while loving someone deeply gives you courage."

~ Lau Tzu

The artillery shells from the German 88's started raining down death and destruction. On January 9, 1945, outside Hatten, France, Elements of the German 125th Regiment of the 21st Panzer Division have penetrated the main line of resistance of the U.S. 1st Battalion, 242nd Infantry Regiment, 42nd Infantry Division. Now the Germans are bombarding the Battalion Command Post (CP). The word is passed, pull back and establish a new CP. Private First Class (PFC) Vito Bertoldo is on guard duty because he couldn't get along with the Company's mess sergeant. When the Battalion Commander asked for volunteers to stay and protect their retreat, Bertoldo enthusiastically volunteered. Three years earlier, Bertoldo was told he was not physically fit for duty because of his poor eyesight. The son of Italian immigrants, he desperately wanted to give back to the country he loved, so he managed to enlist in the Army with the help of a sympathetic doctor. Now, after wheedling his way from stateside duty as a military policeman, he found himself on the front line as the Germans launched Operation Nordwind. This was their last-ditch counter-offensive designed to break the stranglehold of the Allied forces arrayed against them.

Armed with only a machine gun and his rifle, PFC Bertoldo set up in the abandoned CP and waited for the Germans to arrive. Soon, he felt the earth rumble as the German Panzer tanks slowly moved in. Knowing that his machine gun would be useless against them, he patiently waited until the infantry troops showed themselves before opening fire. He spent the next 48 hours, without sleep, holding off the German advance. At one point he stopped their advance for 12 hours while lying down in the middle of the street with a machine gun. He was in full view of the advancing Germans, exposed to the withering 88 mm bombardment from the main guns of the German tanks and held them off with his machine gun. Over a two-day period, Bertoldo survived a point-blank attack from a German 88 mm cannon and another from the main gun of a German Panzer tank.

His Congressional Medal of Honor citation reads in part: "With inspiring bravery and intrepidity M/Sgt. Bertoldo withstood the attack of vastly superior forces for more than 48 hours without rest or relief, time after time escaping death only by the slightest margin while killing at least 40 hostile soldiers and wounding many more during his grim battle against the enemy hordes."[3]

Our history is ripe with stories of courage. From the battle of Thermopylae, where 300 Spartan warriors fought to the last man; to the Hanoi Hilton, the North Vietnamese prisoner of war camp where John McCain turned down an early release, knowing that he would receive more torture, because other POW's had been there longer; to the defense of the U.S. embassy in Benghazi, where four former special forces operators were killed defending the embassy staff from hundreds of insurgents, we have always honored courage.

Heroic courage like that seems almost counterintuitive. After all, we have a well-documented survival mechanism. It is against human nature to put ourselves at risk. As we will soon discover, survival is our most basic fundamental need. Perhaps this recognition that risking oneself for others goes against our nature causes us to honor those who do just that. To determine where courage comes from, we have only to ask those who have demonstrated it to the extreme.

There is a common theme with anyone who has received an award for valor, such as Bronze or Silver Star, a Service Cross or the ultimate recognition in the U.S. Military, the Congressional Medal of Honor. Each recipient is humble about their accomplishment. They believe they did no more than the next man or woman in their unit would have done had they been in the same position. More telling, if asked why they did it, their response is uniformly the same. It wasn't for glory or recognition. In fact, those thoughts never entered their minds, nor did they think about the risk to themselves. They weren't thinking about themselves at all. Instead, they were thinking about their comrades in arms— their teammates. Whether single-handedly holding off a German regiment or jumping on a grenade so the other team members would survive, these men and women cared deeply about others. That caring inspired them to action.

Do You Have What It Takes
to Be a Locked On Leader?

As a locked on leader, we must be similarly outward-focused. Our businesses do not exist to bring ourselves great wealth; they exist to serve others. No business is successful without providing value to others. If you bring enough value to enough people, the wealth will follow. Not just material wealth, but real wealth. The wealth of friends, the wealth of character, the type of wealth we can only get by serving others.

Additionally, no business can maintain sustained success without an inspired and driven team of people working to provide that value. If you are seeking the courage to maintain your integrity, look no further than your heart. If you truly care about your stakeholders you understand that it is in their best interest for you to be consistent and maintain your integrity. When you know, with a certainty, that when you act without integrity your customers, employees, vendors, their employees, and customers may suffer, you will find the courage to act with integrity, even in the face of apparent personal loss. However, you should know and accept on faith that your perceived loss is a canard. I am usually reluctant to speak in absolutes, however, I know that I can safely promise you that by maintaining your integrity in the face of perceived personal loss, your reward will ultimately far exceed any loss.

If you think this may be difficult, don't worry. Like everything else in life, it gets easier with practice. The more consistent you are, the more consistent your team will be. Consistency leads to predictability, which leads to efficiency and growth. If, however, you believe I am completely off base and you believe you can lead a team without demonstrating the consistency of integrity, then read no further. Return the book or give it to someone else because nothing contained in the rest of this book will help you. To inspire others to achieve their potential and become self-actualized, you must care enough about them to find the courage to act with integrity at all times.

PART II

Strategy B4 Tactics

*"Strategy without tactics is the slowest route to victory.
Tactics without strategy is the noise before defeat."*

~ SUN TZU, THE ART OF WAR

Tactics do not exist in a vacuum. Tactics, in the absence of an overarching strategy, are nothing more than busywork. If you are a business owner or manager, chances are you are spending between 50 and 70% of your waking hours working each week. With so little leisure time, it doesn't make sense to engage in activities that aren't designed to achieve specific results. Strategies define your desired results and provide a framework to determine which tactics you should employ. In *Alice's Adventures in Wonderland*, Alice asks the Cheshire Cat which way she should go. The Cat replies that it depends on where you are going. Likewise, the tactics we employ as leaders are directly dependent on our strategic objective(s).

"A battle plan never survives contact with the enemy" is a common military saying. Combat is the ultimate democracy and the enemy gets a vote. However, we frequently don't know their "vote" until it is too late. Referred to as "the fog of war," this is the state of uncertainty that results from a lack of current or complete information. The same condition exists in business, but in many ways, the battlefield of business is more complex.

In war, the ultimate goal is to capture land or prevent the capture of land by a rival. In business, our goal is to capture customers. The land doesn't get a vote, but your customers do. When a field commander understands the strategic objectives, they can adjust their tactics to ensure they achieve the maximum impact of their efforts. In the battle for effective leadership, the other voting members are your employees, their families, your vendors, customers, and others you can't conceive of ahead of time. Each of these gets "a vote" in the battlefield of business and affects your plans. You must adjust your tactics. Like the fog of war, imperfect information may cause additional problems. Therefore, although this book is about tactics, I start by outlining our strategy. Armed with this knowledge, you can adjust your tactics to the changing battlefield of business.

CHAPTER 4

Your Business Strategy

*"Always focus on the front windshield
and not the rearview mirror."*

~ GENERAL COLIN POWELL

I finished flight training and received my wings in October of 1988. I was ordered to the Fighter Squadron 124, the F-14 Tomcat Fleet Replacement Squadron located at Naval Air Station Miramar in San Diego, CA. The F-14 was designed to counter the threat of Soviet strategic bombers. In the event the Cold War turned hot, the Soviets would try to overwhelm a U.S. carrier battle group with a massive quantity of bombers. Since there is a limited number of fighter aircraft available on any aircraft carrier, the U.S. developed a strategy of simultaneous engagements. The F-14 can launch multiple missiles simultaneously. As interceptors, the tactics we employed were all built around the strategy of multiple engagements. However, this was not the same thing as the carrier group's battle strategy. If a Carrier Group Commander employed an ineffective battle strategy, our efforts as interceptors would ultimately be ineffective.

Likewise, your leadership strategy is not the same thing as your business strategy. Without an effective business strategy, where will you lead your team? Imagine yourself as a Scout Leader. You and your troop are in the wilderness. You are an excellent leader; your troop is inspired and efficient. They quickly and efficiently set up and break down the campsite. While hiking between campsites, they naturally and easily help each other over obstacles and work as a smooth and well-oiled machine. The problem is you don't have a final destination, you just wander around the wilderness making camp and breaking it down again. Without a business strategy, you are simply wandering in the wilderness making camp and then breaking it down again. Making money or being profitable is not a strategy, in fact, it shouldn't even be a goal. Being profitable and making money is the result of properly executing a sound business strategy.

In *Locked on Leadership*, we are not going to discuss how to develop a sound business strategy as there are many excellent books on the topic. I am a huge fan of Michael Michalowicz's *The Pumpkin Plan: A Simple Strategy to Grow a Remarkable Business in Any Field*. However, as we will discuss in Chapter 8, you need to create an environment of corporate growth. That requires having a sound business strategy aligned with your company's core values. For closely-held companies, these values are the same as the values of the owner(s).

Personal Values vs. Company Core Values

I spoke with a prospective client about how he could hire better people. I asked him about the core values of his company. He said he had his assistant create them! In other words, his assistant wrote the company's stated values. Imagine what would happen when his personal values came in conflict with these company core values. He would act on his personal values, not the core values of the business. Let's take the example of a company with the stated core value of "Service to Customers" and they center their business strategy around 24-hour service to your clients. If the owner's personal over-arching core value is "Family," the owner will choose family over serving the customer when it's not convenient. By doing so, it causes all kinds of problems. First and foremost, this erodes the client's faith in the company. After all, if the company's strategy is built around serving its clients, then the marketing and sales process undoubtedly reflects this value. When the owner fails to honor this implied commitment to clients, they can't help but wonder where else they were misled. Additionally, the owner loses credibility with the team and potentially undermines some of their efforts. This sends a subliminal, yet powerful, message that the company's leadership can't be trusted. When employees lose faith in their leadership, they don't feel safe. If your team doesn't feel safe, group cohesiveness breaks down. Simply put, you just put a giant roadblock on the path to team members realizing their full potential.

For closely-held companies, the company's values are the owner's values. If there is more than one owner, they need to develop the company's values as a group to ensure there is no conflict with any one owner's personal values. In my experience, partnerships only work when all the principals share the same or similar values.

LOCKED ON VALUES EXERCISE

1. Make a list of everything important to you. If you search the Internet for "list of values," it might help you think of things that are not top of mind. At this point, it is better to have too many than too few.

2. Divide your list into three groups labeled A, B, C with the most important values in the A group and the least important values in the C group. If you aren't sure which group a value belongs in, place it in B.

3. Eliminate the C group.

4. Repeat this until you have 10 or fewer values.

5. Prioritize your remaining values from 1 to 10 (or however many you have). If you get stuck trying to prioritize two values, ask yourself when a conflict happens, which one would prevail? Your gut may pull you one way and your head another. Listen to your gut. Your head is trying to rationalize a decision, but your gut is how you feel. Ultimately, you will do as you feel, not as you think. That's why it's important to be honest with yourself.

6. If there are multiple owners, each partner should do this separately. If you own a corporation, the directors of the corporation should go through this exercise. Then look for overlap and possible conflicts and work to resolve them.

7. Once each owner or director has written down their personal values, look for the commonalities. Ideally, there should be five top five values that all agree upon.

I've worked with companies where the owners don't share common values. It always degenerates to infighting that ultimately hurt the company. Furthermore, the CEO of a corporation or the Managing Member of an LLC must embody all of the company's values or their decisions will not align with that of the board of directors.

Core values are the lynchpin that high-performing teams rely on to attract and keep the best possible talent. In addition, they become a litmus test to use with all of your policies and procedures. If a policy contradicts or undermines a core value, change it. If you don't, your policies will undermine your values and the values will become nothing more than words on a wall or web page. '

Locked On Tip

Revisit your company's values annually and make sure they are still germane and your policies and procedures reflect them.

CHAPTER 5

Leadership Strategy

"If sovereign and subject are in accord, put division between them."
~ Sun Tzu, The Art of War

I got my first job at the age of 14. My dad was a school teacher, and my mom had the most important job in the world—staying home and raising my two brothers and me. I grew up in a house with an abundance of love but little money. As soon as I was old enough to work legally, I got a part-time job as a busboy in a Chinese restaurant. The owners didn't exactly have a training program, and at this point in my life, I had not paid any attention to restaurant workers. I remember clearly not knowing what to do. Although I did what I was told, I didn't do anything I wasn't explicitly told to do. Unsurprisingly, the job didn't last. I suspect they got tired of having to tell me what to do.

My next job was as a dishwasher in another Chinese restaurant. They showed me where the busboys stack the dirty dishes, how to clean them, and where to put them once done. Then they set me to work. As the dinner rush began, the dishes started stacking up. I attacked the pile with a vigor. Every time I came close to clearing the dirty dishes, a fresh batch would arrive. Like Sisyphus and his rock, I persevered attempting to clear the dirty dishes before my shift ended. Unfortunately, my goal was just as unobtainable as this ancient Greek's, so instead of leaving when the time came, I stayed at my station, pushing the rock up the hill, only to see it slide back down as they cleared the next table or the cooks needed clean woks, pans and utensils again. I was constantly pushing the rock again and again. On several occasions, I worked clear through until closing. Fifteen years later, as a junior officer in the United States Navy, I saw sailors report to our squadron demonstrating the traits of both versions of the young me.

The first version of the young me is what I call "the robot." We have all worked with this person. When they arrive at work, the first thing they do is jabber jaw with their coworkers waiting for instructions from a supervisor. In the absence of any direction, they stand idle. Once you give them input they do as they are told. The better robots will attack their task energetically, happy to have direction, and something to do. Others are more lacka-daisical; their only thought is to pass the time so they can collect a paycheck. In either case, our robots can only follow direction. Some don't even have the ability to discern when something goes wrong. They continue to execute their last instruction set unless circumstances arise that prevent them from working. Then, the least capable of them, simply shut down. You only become aware of an issue when you find them smoking a cigarette looking puz-zled because they can't do what they were told. If you're lucky, your robot may notify you of the problem but don't count on it.

In the second version of the young me, we have a highly motivated, self-starting teammate. Unlike the robot, when they arrive at work, they dive right in, even if their shift hasn't officially started. You will frequently find them initiating tasks on their own, even if they were not specifically assigned to do so. They understand their role in your organization, how they fit in, how they affect your work flow, how their duties interact with the rest of the team, and they see the "Big Picture." If they come to you with a problem they frequently have a suggested solution and are just looking for permission to implement it. They are even known to solve problems without asking. This worker is completely self-actualized and you only need to point them in the direction you want them to go, and they will do what it takes to get there.

Finding the Best Employee

The two versions of me don't represent all of the possible teammates you will encounter. There is a continuum of team members, with the robot at one end and the self-actualized coworker at the other. Over the years, I've encountered numerous business owners whose business strategy is to "hire the best help available." They are on a perpetual quest for the "self-actualized employee." I constantly hear the complaint that good, much less great, employees aren't around, can't be found or are already employed. This is a universal problem regardless of location.

The problem is there are not that many self-actualized workers available in any one industry. To truly understand the magnitude of the problem, I have to delve into some basic statistics. If we look at distribution of talent, we know that 68% of the population is centered around the average. This is defined as one standard deviation. Since 68% is roughly two out of every three job applicants, then two out of three people who apply for a job are simply average. This means one out of three applicants are either above or below average. Statistically, we would expect an even split so one out of six job applicants are good or great at what they do and one out of six are bad or terrible at what they do. All things being equal, this means that you have at best one-in-six chance of randomly finding an employee that is at least "good." Since most of the good or better applicants are probably already employed, your actual chances are much less than that. If you are looking for "great" employees, your chances are even smaller. Ninety-five percent of the population are within two standard deviations of average so you only have one in 40 chances of randomly hiring a "great" employee. If you are looking for a "superstar," someone greater than three standard deviations from the norm, your chances fall to one in 200.

Let us put this in perspective. According to the U.S. Census Bureau, the 2016 estimated population for the New York-Newark Combined Statistical Area is just over 20 million, 11 million of which are of employment age. Of those 11 million potential employees, only 1.77 million are statistically "good" at what they do, a mere 277,000 would be considered "great," and there are only 55,400 "superstars." That's everyone who is of working age. How many of them are going to have the skills and desire to do whatever position you may be looking for? Of those, how many are actually looking for work? The odds of hiring a "good," much less "great," employee are statistically insignificant. If you're relying on hiring "good" or "great" employees as a strategy, you are setting yourself up for failure. This is a terrible business strategy and an even worse leadership strategy.

Leadership Makes a Difference

You can see that hiring the best is a doomed strategy for many reasons. Even if you find "good" or "great" team members, there is no guarantee they will perform for you if you don't understand how to lead them. History is replete with ineffective leaders of great teams that failed. In the American Revolutionary War, the Continental Army was greatly outclassed during the initial fighting. The British Army was a competent, highly-trained army with centuries of experience. At the time of the American Revolution, the British Empire spanned the world. With territory in all six habitable continents and on islands in all the great seas and oceans, the British Military had more talent and experience to draw upon than all the colonies combined. However, even in the early days of the Revolution, when colonial leadership had not fully come into its ascendancy, the colonial military saw strategic wins over the British Army. As the American Military Leadership, under the tutelage of Generals Washington and Von Steuben, came into its own, the "mediocre" American soldier was able to defeat the highly trained and skilled British Regular. The difference was leadership.

In more recent times we have seen a similar pattern. Our Special Operations Command has the greatest warriors in history. These soldiers are the best of the best, easily in the top 1% of all warriors since the beginning of time. Yet in the early days of the war in Iraq, these highly trained, skilled, and motivated operators were unable to achieve their strategic objective. This had nothing to do with their skill, but was the result of the leadership early on in the war. In his book, *One Mission: How Leaders Build a Team of Teams*, former NAVY SEAL and Aide de Camp to General Stanley McCrystal, Chris Fussell, details how a change in culture empowered U.S. Special Forces Operators to achieve amazing gains against the insurgency. The difference was not in the tactics, nor the overall military strategy. The same group of operators, with the same strategic objectives, increased their effectiveness 300% according to Fussell. The difference was the leadership of Major General McCrystal.

Leadership skill will affect teams of any size, not just enterprise-size organizations like the Special Operations Command. Sailors attempting to qualify as SEALS are divided into small teams of six or seven called "Boat Teams." In their book, *Extreme Ownership: How U.S. Navy Seals Lead and Win*, Jocko Willick and Leaf Babin detail how swapping the leaders of the top- and worst-performing boat crew propelled the worst crew instantly to top performers. This was due to the new leader's ability to lead and inspire, not his physical prowess.

The significance of leadership in creating high-performance teams has also been conclusively proven in a study by Google. In 2009, their "People Analytics Group" performed a study of managers called "Project Oxygen." The study classified managers based on a compilation of data from two sources—the manager's performance review scores and the results of Google's own "Googlegeist Survey." In this survey, 90% of Google's employees evaluated how they felt about career development, perks, benefits, and company culture. Google found the top 25% of managers had lower turnover and higher-performing teams than those in the bottom quartile. Team members under the top-ranked managers scored higher in all Googlegeist dimensions including innovation, work-life balance, and career development.[4]

So, if leadership is the deciding factor between high- and low-performing teams, what can we do, as leaders, to make sure we are as effective as possible? We know that hiring the best is not a viable strategy. The question is: how can we "make" our team the best and what strategy should we employ to do this? The answer is in the continuum of team members we referred to earlier. We know we would rather employ the self-actualized team member and not the robot.

A Moving Story

We are starting our weekly 7:30 am Friday office meeting. One of my move coordinators, think inside sales rep, we will call him Rock, walks into the conference room. His affect is sullen; he's looking down, and not smiling. I assume it is because he is five minutes late for a meeting that everyone knows starts on time. Meetings starting late were a problem when I first joined the company but not anymore. The first time I started the meeting on time

I was the only person in the room, and I held everyone accountable for the information I put out even though they weren't there. It had been a long time since anyone showed up late without a good reason. The only acceptable reason was they were dealing with a customer crisis. On this day Rock was late.

As I continue the meeting, Rock does not engage in his usual banter. Rock is a clever and funny man. Uneducated but with a quick mind, he's a hard worker. When I first started at the moving company, I don't think he trusted me because I had never worked in the industry before. For my part, I couldn't believe he was booking moves as he sounded unprofessional. Many of our customers were affluent and he spoke with a ghetto patois. As we started working together we gained some mutual respect. Ultimately, I came to rely heavily on Rock as he made good, sound decisions, was a willing and able worker, and I could count on him. However, during this particular meeting, we were still in the process of developing our mutual respect. I was miffed that he was late.

After the meeting was over, I asked him to stick around. His less than enthusiastic response grated on my nerves. After all, he was the one that was late, not me. I wanted to ask him, "Why the crappy attitude?" However, I remembered a lesson I learned when I was an Ensign in the Navy.

I'm in my first training squadron, Fixed Wing Training Squadron 10 (VT-10) in Pensacola, Fl. On this day, I was standing watch as the Junior Squadron Duty Officer. This was my first watch in this command. My job was simple, I answered the phone and radio and let the Squadron Duty Officer know if anything went wrong. This was usually a quiet watch and today was no exception. During my watch a salty and crusty Chief Petty Officer came into the Ready Room and we started chatting. At some point, he said, "…let me ask you something, sir. Let's pretend you're the Branch Officer, and I'm your Chief. The Skipper asks you to get a complete inventory of all the tools we are supposed to have. What do you do?"

I started to detail the steps on completing this task. That's when he interrupted me and said, "No sir, that is wrong, what you should do is turn to me and say, 'Chief, get me a tools inventory,' and leave the rest to me. It's my job to get things done." I asked him, "If it's your job to get things done, what's my job?" He responded, "Sir, your job is to take care of your sailors, make sure everything is good outside the shop so they can focus on their job without distractions. If they are having trouble with their pay, kids, or anything else they'll be thinking about that. Our job is dangerous enough without having someone distracted by stuff going on at home. Your job is to make sure that doesn't happen."

In a nanosecond, the memory of this exchange flashed in my head. Instead of reprimanding Rock for being late, I asked him, "What's going on? It's not like you to be late." That's when he shared with me that one of his daughters was diagnosed with a severe health issue. I recognized immediately that this is one of those situations the Chief was talking about. Rock was understandably distracted and off his game. He told me about all the upcoming doctor visits. The Chief's words, "take care of them..." echoed in my mind. I reassured Rock his job was not in jeopardy and he could take time off as needed. I saw the weight lift a little off his shoulders. He shared that his daughter is not on his health plan and he doesn't know how he can afford the doctor visits. I saw my opportunity. With the shade of that old Chief looking over my shoulder, I made some calls to our insurance broker. I explained the situation, and through some legerdemain maneuvering, Rock's daughter was on his insurance by the end of the week.

The change in Rock after this event was enormous and gratifying to see. Although I have always tried to do right by my employees with fair policies, this was the most dramatic turnaround I had ever witnessed. Rock had always been a conscientious team member, but immediately he elevated his game even more. He was no longer content with doing what was asked. He became proactive and started solving problems on his own unless he needed my advice. He moved up the continuum towards self-actualization, which is the need to become what you are capable of being.

What caused this sudden movement up the continuum towards self-actualization? The answer can be found in the work of famed psychologist Abraham Maslow. Maslow (1908 -1970) focused his study of Psychology on the realization of human potential. In 1954, he published *Motivation and Personality*, where he first unveiled his Hierarchy of Needs. Maslow theorized that humans have five intrinsic needs that must be met sequentially. He showed how we are driven to meet the lower-level or more basic needs before we strive to meet the higher-level needs. In fact, Maslow theorized that the higher-level needs won't even be felt until the lower-level needs are satisfied. Furthermore, each subsequent level actually reinforces and strengthens the level below.

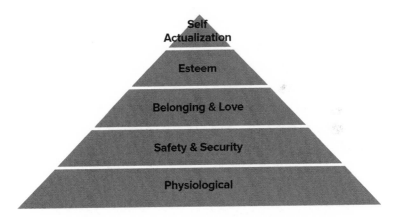

The five different levels of need postulated by Maslow are:

1. Physiological
2. Safety and security
3. Belonging and love
4. Esteem
5. Self-actualization

With a little thought, I think we would all agree with his assessment. If any of us were stranded in the middle of the wilderness, our first thought would be to secure water and food (in that order), then protect ourselves from extremes of heat or cold. These are our physiological needs.

The next thing we want to do is protect ourselves from harm. We need to find a secure place to sleep, fashion weapons, erect a more permanent shelter to protect ourselves from weather, predators, and fellow humans.

As humans, we are pack animals. We work better and are much more effective in groups by design. Our physiology has evolved to reinforce this need. Nature has provided us with hormones, such as oxytocin, the hormone responsible for feelings of trust and intimacy and arginine vasopressin (AVP) which stimulates, amongst other things, group cooperation. The next level in Maslow's Hierarchy is "Belonging and Love." In other words, we have a need to belong to a group and be loved. You've heard there is safety in numbers. Being part of a group makes us safer and it is easier to meet our mutual physiological needs. If we are sick or injured, others in the group can provide for us.

The next need Maslow identified is esteem. This refers to both internal esteem (self-esteem), and how we are viewed by others (external esteem). Again, this makes sense when viewed against our life experiences. In groups, we want to and actually need to know where/how we fit in, and what role we fill in the group. We want to be appreciated for our contributions and get immense satisfaction fulfilling our role within the group. The more esteem we feel, both internally and externally, the stronger our bond to the group and the more effective we become. This also facilitates our feelings of love and belonging, reinforcing the lower-level need. This effect cascades down and the group is stronger.

Finally, only after our esteem needs are met can we look internally and start to reach for our maximum personal potential. Buoyed by the esteem of our peers, feeling loved and like we belong, we find the courage to stretch ourselves. We reach for greatness knowing our efforts are appreciated and the group will be stronger for it.

When I told Rock that his job was not in jeopardy, I sent a powerful message. I reinforced all four of the lower-order needs. I assured him his job was not in jeopardy, simultaneously meeting his physiological need by allowing him to continue to obtain food and shelter and his security and safety needs by assuring him he had job security. I reinforced his sense of belonging when I subliminally informed him that he is important to the group. I reinforced his esteem by valuing his efforts enough to work around and through his personal problems. His response was to strive to reach his personal potential and to grow in his job. In other words, by fulfilling his Belonging and Esteem needs I allowed him to focus on Self-Actualization.

Locked On Tip

Never discuss attitude with a teammate. You can't read their mind. Discuss the behaviors you see and hear; they will reveal their underlying issues to you.

Herein is your strategy for Leadership success. If you strive to move your team members up Maslow's Hierarchy you will create a high-performing team, regardless of what their talents and skills are at the beginning.

It is important to understand that while Maslow's Hierarchy doesn't always have to be met in a serial fashion, our needs can be met in parallel as long as there are no gaps in the hierarchy. Imagine if you came upon a starving man in the wilderness and announced that you were going to join him. If you simply encouraged and cared for him, your efforts would be futile as he needs food and protection from the elements. Without meeting his physiological needs or safety needs, the sense of belonging you offer would have no meaning. However, if the two of you found food and protected each other, then by joining together you would simultaneously meet the first three tiers of Maslow's Hierarchy.

The other important insight into Maslow's Hierarchy is that the way we meet our higher-order needs must reinforce and strengthen our abilities to meet our lower-order needs. However, we will sacrifice higher-order needs, if necessary, to meet lower-order needs. For example, if we become ill, we realize it would be more difficult to provide food for ourselves. So, to protect ourselves from illness, we don't go out into the cold rain to hunt, a safety need. As a result, assuming we have enough food to eat, we are better able to provide food, a physiological need. However, if we are hungry, and it is raining, we may still hunt because food is more important than our need for safety.

To become a locked on leader, understanding Maslow's Hierarchy is crucial. You don't need to have a PhD in Psychology, but a basic understanding of Maslow's theory will allow you to evaluate your efforts as a leader. It is an invaluable tool that provides the framework for a comprehensive leadership model that enables you to improvise with a high degree of certainty that your efforts will be fruitful. The reason for this is simple; Maslow's needs are anthropologically driven and hard-wired into us as a matter of survival. In short, survival trumps satisfaction. When we remove the barriers to survival, we open the door to individual satisfaction. When our team members are satisfied, they are more likely to be self-actualized.

Armed with a solid leadership strategy, we turn our attention to the tactics we need to achieve our strategic goals. Before going into battle, unit commanders prepare the battlefield to maximize the effectiveness of their planned tactics. Sometimes they alter terrain features, lay out tank traps, identify gun emplacements, and remove obstructions to the field of fire. Your leadership tactics also require proper preparation.

PART III

Preparation

*"In preparing for battle I have always found that
plans are useless, but planning is indispensable."*

~ DWIGHT D. EISENHOWER

The key to successfully completing any mission or under-
taking is advance preparation. This holds true for simple
projects like painting a wall in your house or complex
undertakings, like Operation Overlord, the amphibious assault
on the beaches of Normandy in World War II.

If you are painting a wall, you may be tempted to go to the
hardware store, purchase the paint, brushes, rollers and tarps, and
then go back home and start slapping paint on the wall. No matter how carefully you paint, once you are done, you will notice
imperfections. Blemishes and holes will stand out, the old color
may bleed through, and the paint may not stick or take well. Why?

You didn't prepare the wall properly. A good paint job starts with getting the wall ready to paint by cleaning, patching, and sanding.

A complicated mission, like the invasion of Normandy, is no different. General Eisenhower could have simply said, "Load the boats, let's hit the beaches!" However, if he did that, I would probably be writing this book in German, if at all. To successfully invade France, Eisenhower needed to know:

- where the German troops were stationed
- where the obstacles and mines on the beaches were located
- which bridges could hold their tanks and which could not
- where the anti-tank ditches were situated
- which cliffs could be scaled
- which bridges should be blown up and which ones should be protected and much more.

The same could be said for the tactics of leadership. I could simply give you the words to say, the activities to engage in, but without the proper foundation, without the preparation, your efforts will be fruitless.

Tactical Leadership is the day-to-day behaviors that create conditions for each and every member to achieve self-actualization. These practices are grounded in meeting your team's Love and Belonging Needs (level 3) and Esteem Needs (level 4). The preparation lies in the first two levels of Maslow's Hierarchy: Physiological Needs (level 1) and Safety and Security Needs (level 2).

CHAPTER 6

First Tier Physiology

"Be an example to your men, in your duty and in private life. Never spare yourself and let your troops see that you don't in your endurance of fatigue and privation. Always be tactful and well-mannered. Avoid excessive sharpness or harshness of voice, which usually indicates the man who has shortcomings of his own to hide."

~ German Field Marshal Erwin Rommel

The good news is you are already fulfilling the first level on Maslow's Hierarchy when you hire a new team member. It would be a mistake, however, to think there is no way to optimize this process. While sound leadership will elevate any team, why not start with the best talent possible? This may seem at odds with my earlier assertion that hiring the best is not a sound business strategy. Let me assure you, it is not. Hiring "the best" you can get is not a good strategy, but it is an excellent and sound tactic.

According to Gallup's 2017 State of the American Workplace, half of workers in the United States are not engaged and another

16% are actively-disengaged.[5] Put another way, only one out of three American workers are engaged at the workplace and the cost of employee non-engagement is huge. According to Gallup, workplace engagement affects absenteeism, turnover, shrinkage, employee safety, patient safety, quality, customer satisfaction, production, and sales. Not having engaged employees costs the average company about 17% in profits!

The challenge comes in how we define "the best" candidates. Most managers only consider the specific skills necessary to technically fulfill the job, and their gut reaction to the candidate. This is not sufficient. According to one study entitled, *"Validity and Utility of Alternative Predictors of Job Performance,"*[6] when a manager hires based solely on an interview and resume review, only about one out of seven new hires work out. There are many reasons for this. Most interviews fail to explore a candidate's values or motivators. Many companies discuss their culture but do it to attract the candidate. Rarely do companies explore if there truly is a cultural fit between the applicant and the company. Culture is offered as an enticement but it should really be a barrier.

It doesn't help that most job seekers, especially if they are unemployed and seeking work, are not as discriminating as they could be. Remember Maslow? To fulfill our first need (physiological), we rely on employment to eat, find housing, and obtain clothes. Since fifty percent of adult Americans have no savings, when we are unemployed, we are not thinking about safety, love and affection, or esteem. We're only concerned with where we will get our next meal.

The Difference Between Looking for a Job When Employed vs. Unemployed

Looking for a job is a completely different experience for the already employed job seeker. Candidates have a baseline to start with—their current job. No matter how bad it is, they would be foolish to move to a worse situation. If employed, a job seeker's first tier physiological needs are met so the higher-order needs become more important. Employed job seekers will look towards perceived job security, company values and how much recognition to expect for future contributions to a new employer, in that order. Their decision is dependent on which needs are not being met by their current employer.

Consider that you need to fill a position and are interviewing four candidates. Candidate A is working at a company that is downsizing. Candidate B is working for a stable company but feels like an outsider there. Candidate C has been with their current employer for a long time but feels undervalued by his boss. Candidate D has been unemployed for 11 months, is running out of unemployment benefits, and has no savings to fall back on. Under these conditions, Candidate A is concerned with your company's stability and growth. Candidate B will be interested in your company's values and culture. Candidate C will be interested in your recognition programs. Unless Candidate D has multiple offers, they just want a job. All of these candidates have their own self-interest at heart.

There is a mutual responsibility between job applicants and hiring managers to explore if the values and mores of the company and candidate are in alignment. A bad hiring decision can be debilitating for both the applicant and the company. In addition, as a leader, you are obligated to your team to set each and every member up for success. We'll talk more about this in the next chapter, but the process starts when you hire a new team member.

Defining "The Best"

Since we can't rely on hard skills to assess how good a team member a candidate will be, we need another way to determine who is "the best" candidate. I have my clients evaluate their candidates using the following criteria (shown in order of importance):

1. Values
2. Cultural fit

3. Behavioral style
4. Emotional intelligence (EQ)
5. Soft skills
6. Hard skills

As we discussed in Chapter 4, values are how we make decisions. Just like business partners need to share common values, team members do as well. Diversity is powerful because it brings many different experiences and viewpoints to enhance creativity and expose the team to new ideas. But diversity in values brings nothing but conflict. However, you can't simply ask a job candidate if they share your values because they may not be candid with their answer—especially if they are desperate for a job. Therefore, we need to uncover their values during the interview by asking questions that don't have a clear, correct answer but reveal the candidate's values. To do this, give a scenario that has conflicting demands and then ask what they would do. One of my clients, who provides outsourced IT services to businesses, asks the following question of prospective technicians.

Scenario: It's 4:45 pm and you are the only one in the office when the phone rings. The caller is a smaller client, not one of the top clients the company typically caters to. The caller states that they have a new employee starting tomorrow at 8:00 am and they need a computer workstation and phone set up with all the passwords set and applications loaded that the new employee will need. They have the equipment on site. The caller further states they know they dropped the ball as their request should have been made a week ago per their agreement with your company.

You realize that you will have to drive to the client's office to get everything done. At this time of the evening, it is a 45-minute drive and you will need at least two hours to get the work done. In addition, a review of their file shows they are on a 9 to 5 contract and any work after five o'clock will be billable. Compounding the issue, you just received a memo stating no overtime is authorized without a manager's approval. You ask the client to hold while you "check on a few things" and you try to reach a manager, but there is no answer. What do you do?

I love this question because I get to see how the candidate thinks and prioritizes. In other words, it demonstrates their critical thinking skills. We do this as a role play so I can move them towards the conflict. For example, the candidate might say something like, "You said they are starting tomorrow at eight, does that mean they need their computer and phone right away or do they need to do paperwork first?" This demonstrates creative thinking and is possibly a good solution. I'll answer the question, "No, they've completed their paperwork and need their computer." I make sure they never get ahold of their manager and have to make the decision on their own. I'm looking to see if they will take care of the customer. This company's culture supports and rewards independent decision-making.

As you can see, the correct answer to this question is dependent on the company's values. I recommend coming up with multiple questions like this for each value. I typically ask these value questions towards the end of the interview when the candidate is tired and less on guard. You will then get more candid answers.

Locked on Value Interview Questions Exercise

1. Come up with two or three conflicting values for each of your company's values. The conflicting values should not be obviously bad values. For example, stealing is obviously bad. It is best if the conflicting value has a solid business purpose like "following company directives" in the above scenario.

2. Create a scenario where the correct choice depends on your actual value. Play devil's advocate and ask yourself if your value was otherwise, is there a good answer in the scenario?

3. Develop your own answer to the exercise keeping in mind there may be more than one solution. In the scenario above, the technician could either go to the client's office now or go in the morning at 6 am (if the client says they can meet them) and work until 3 pm to avoid overtime.
4. Develop a list of possible questions the candidate might ask and then answer them so you move the candidate in the direction of the conflict.
5. Test the scenario on existing employees to see what they come up with, modify the scenario as necessary.

Different Behavior Styles

We all have our own behavioral style. This was recognized as far back as 400 B.C. when Hippocrates described how people behaved based on the geographic terrain in which they were raised.[7] In 1928, William Moulton Marston published, *Emotions of Normal People* where he described our behaviors as "…behaving along two axes with their actions tending to be active or passive depending upon the individual's perception of the environment as either antagonistic or favorable."[8] These two axes create four quadrants representing different behavioral styles. Marston's work has evolved into modern-day DISC theory. DISC describes the four behavior styles as follows:

Dominance, the way we prefer to respond to problems
Influence, how we attempt to influence people
Steadiness, how we deal with the changes of pace in our environment
Compliance, how we approach procedures

These traits are measured on a scale of 0 to 100, however, the nature of the scale is deceptive. Someone who registers a 0 for a trait doesn't mean they don't exhibit any characteristics of the trait, rather they exhibit all of the opposite characteristics of the trait. For example, someone with a 100 in Influence would be described as optimistic and trusting of other people. Someone with a 0 in Influence wouldn't be indifferent to others. They would be pessimistic and distrusting of others. A score of 50 is considered moderate. The farther away from 50, the stronger the trait is present, either positively or negatively. Our behavioral style is a combination of all four traits.

In every company, each position complements specific DISC behavioral styles. For example, a staff accountant performing auditing functions would be best suited for someone with high -C- or Compliance traits. If they are required to spend a great deal of time on a specific project you may want to see high -S- or Steadiness as well. If they are working alone, you would not want someone with high -I- or Influence characteristics.

On the other hand, a Chief Financial Officer position requires a different set of characteristics. C-level executives need to develop consensus so someone with high -I- characteristics would be ·beneficial. Steadiness characteristics may depend on the type of company. A young, nimble, and agile company, like many tech startups, will have a different requirement for a CFO's -S- characteristics than a well-established company such as an insurance underwriter.

This doesn't mean we can't adapt to the job requirements by modifying our behavior. However, when someone changes their behavior from their natural behaviors, they put themselves under internal stress. Under normal circumstances, we can usually manage this stress. But with external pressures, the stress can multiply beyond our ability to manage. When this happens, our behaviors revert to our natural state. If the adapted behavior is required for job performance, then performance suffers, usually when it is needed the most.

I am a perfect case in point. My Compliance is a 36, this indicates that I am loose with compliance and details, not extremely organized. My adapted -C- is a 66, fairly strongly compliant and organized. Normally, my office is relatively tidy and orderly.

However, if you saw me finishing up a project while up against an intense deadline, my desk would look like a tornado hit it. Organizing my desk takes energy. Since my strongest DISC characteristic is a 76 -D- my natural and preferred behavioral mode is to put my energy towards solving problems. At this point, the energy it takes to organize is not available. Like all of us, when faced with extraordinary pressure, I revert to my natural behavioral style. In my case, this means that organization goes out the door.

As a leader, one of your primary responsibilities is to set up each of your team members for success. According to a study conducted by TTI Success Insights[9], researchers were able to identify entrepreneurs 60% of the time when using DISC assessments. When adding a second assessment measuring a person's motivators, that went up to 80%. By adding a third assessment, their success rate went up to 94%. The implication of this research is staggering. The biggest cost of a failed hire is lost time. When you have a vision and a plan for your company, the longer it takes to put together your team, the longer it takes to realize your dream. When my clients are looking to hire for any position, I always recommend they benchmark the position. This allows us to figuratively build the perfect teammate. We determine the behavioral style, motivators and soft skills the position requires, then we measure applicants against these requirements. This allows us to explore areas of potential weaknesses and determine whether these weaknesses can be lived with or mitigated through training or other means. If they can, then the candidate is a contender for hiring, if not, they are less attractive as prospective teammates.

Locked On Tip

Give your team the best chance of success by hiring members whose behaviors, motivators, and soft skills are ideally suited for the job. This is the best predictor of job success.

CHAPTER 7

Second Tier Safety

"A man who has no consideration for the needs
of his men ought never to be given command."

~ Napoleon Bonaparte

In 1995, my first job after leaving the Navy was working for a small telecommunications company in San Diego. To build a better-functioning team, the owner decided we would have a regular company happy hour. One Monday each month we would go to a local pub at 4 pm. Hourly employees got paid from 4 pm to 5 pm. The first month, the company bought appetizers and beer and it was well attended. The second month, we were responsible for our own food and beverages and not everyone showed up. That's when the owner said, "If you don't want to go, then you have to stay at the office." Since the employees would rather sit at a bar than be at work, everyone went to the happy hour. The owner thought that this would create an opportunity to bond and foster loyalty to the company, it did anything but. After two months, the happy hour was referred to as "mandatory fun." For those employees that were not sitting with the owner, it turned into a bitch session. Hate and discontent festered and grew. Does this mean that company-sponsored bonding events are a bad idea? Far from it. The problem was that the owner was trying to create a sense of community, Maslow's third tier of love and belonging, without first attending to the employees' second tier safety needs.

What are "Safety Needs" in a business?

In 2013, I was the President of a moving company in San Diego. One day, as I drove into the moving company's yard, I saw one of our trucks heading out to the street. There was a driver and passenger inside the cab and an individual standing on the step to the cab, holding onto the mirror. I saw red! A couple recent accidents cost the company thousands of dollars and now these guys were putting someone's life at risk. I stopped them and told the guy on the outside to get down, the other two to park the truck, and everyone to meet me in the conference room. To say I was angry was calling the Sahara a sandbox. I parked my car, informed the Operations Manager what I saw, and asked him to join us. A few minutes later everyone was in the conference room but the driver. I found him in the warehouse getting ready to leave. When I told him I needed him in the conference room now, he replied he would be late for his class. He was a Psychology major in a local college. My blood already percolating, I replied, "I don't care about your class. If you don't get in the conference room, don't come back!" Grumbling, "That's the problem, you don't care about us," he joined the others.

I proceeded with a heated monologue (did I mention I was furious?) on how what they did was incredibly stupid. I ranted that the guy on the step was risking his life as people have died in similar fashion. By doing something so stupid they put the company at risk, and therefore, the livelihood of over 50 people, including the owner, who they all liked. He had risked hundreds of thousands of dollars of his own money to build this business and provide them all jobs. I then said, "You may not care about your friends and coworkers, but I do, just like I care about *you* and that is why I am so furious!"

After the meeting wrapped up, I asked the Operations Manager to keep an eye on the three of them. I was concerned that my tirade may have an unintended negative effect. The opposite happened. All three movers became more productive and more safety-conscience. By showing them my concern for their safety was greater than my need for them to like me, I created an atmosphere that strengthened their bond to the company and their coworkers.

This story illustrates why physical safety is the second level of Maslow's Hierarchy. To have a high-performing team, physical safety is an absolute requirement. There is an emphasis on personal safety when the military trains our soldiers, sailors, airmen, and marines. The job is dangerous enough without carelessness, much less recklessness, adding to the danger. If you are in a high-risk industry such as logging, roofing, or structural steel, then an emphasis on safety is critical. All of these are in the top 10 occupations for fatalities in 2014 according to the Bureau of Labor Statistics. In addition to the compelling moral argument that we must be responsible for each other, it makes good business sense. Though few of the high-risk jobs are commensurately high paying, these workers are all high skilled. However, in the U.S., safety regulations ensure businesses of any size follow the safety rules. But physical safety is not the only safety consideration. In addition, employees are concerned with another form of safety—job security.

If you have ever worked at a company that was "downsizing" or "right-sizing" you know the stress and fear that goes along with job insecurity. People do all sorts of strange and creative things to protect themselves when they believe their job is at risk. Their focus turns to keeping their jobs and not accomplishing the company's mission. On the surface, these two objectives may seem aligned, but in reality, they are not. Employees that are at risk are less willing to admit mistakes and faults and some may actively hide them. These problems may seem small but like a wound from a grazing bullet, if left untreated they can become infected and may threaten life or limb. Similarly, when mistakes or errors in business go uncorrected, they can grow into huge customer service, or even PR, nightmares. According to David Sirota in *The Enthusiastic Employee: How Companies Profit By Giving Workers What They Want,* people have three desires while at work: equity, achievement, and camaraderie[10]. Equity is defined as "...To be treated justly in relation to the basic conditions of employment."[11] Sirota further refines the definition to include "Physiological, such as having a safe working environment..." and "Economic, such as having a reasonable degree of job security..."[12]

Since job security is a goal of employees and a requirement to advance team members up Maslow's Hierarchy towards self-actualization, why don't we have a policy of not firing someone regardless of performance? Wouldn't this create an environment of "Safety" and pave the way for creating an environment of love and acceptance? Not exactly.

In 2011, I was hired by the San Diego moving company I previously mentioned as the Vice President. The founder, CEO, and President was an old friend of mine. He is a smart, successful entrepreneur with an MBA from Cal Berkley. When I joined the company, it was the preeminent local moving company in San Diego. He was on his way to becoming the premier agent for one of the top van lines in the country. Shortly before I started there, one of his customer service representatives was misbehaving. She spent most of her time socializing with coworkers while ignoring her duties. My friend, the owner, talked to her about her behavior but there were never any consequences. Her behavior devolved and socializing became flirting. One day she made a sexual proposition to two movers, simultaneously. As a result, the owner finally terminated her employment. She was completely surprised when he let her go. She said, "I didn't think you fired anybody."

Although he did not have a non-termination policy, his managerial tactics created a de facto policy of job security. In Chapter 9, we will discuss in detail why this policy failed. Such a policy has the opposite of its intended effect. It costs you valuable employees and ultimately your bottom line.

Your Safety & Security Flight Plan

For safety reasons, when pilots prepare to fly a plane, they file a flight plan. Besides identifying information for the aircraft, flight plans include your proposed route, time in route, number of people on board, fuel, and alternate landing sites along the route. This flight plan ensures pilots consider all the factors before getting into an aircraft. It also provides emergency responders some idea where to look for them should they have a problem. In other words, they enhance safety.

In business, just like flying a plane, to increase the feeling of safety and security for our team, we need to have our own flight plan.

Five critical elements in your safety and security flight plan include:

1. Environment of Corporate Growth
2. Clear Job Descriptions
3. Simple Metrics
4. Formalized Training
5. A Defined Career Path

1. Environment of Corporate Growth

While flying for the US Navy, we would practice air combat maneuvering, also known as ACM. Often, two adversaries, attempting to gain a firing position, would find themselves literally flying in circles, each aircraft chasing the other's tail maneuvering for a kill shot. Imagine two children chasing each other playing tag. They run in circles until one eventually tires from expending energy and loses speed. Then, the other one wins by tagging the tired one. In ACM, the jets also expend energy and lose speed. Unlike the children, they can regain speed to either stay ahead or catch up, by descending in altitude while turning. Essentially trading altitude for air speed. As you can imagine, this can't go on forever. Eventually, you run out of altitude and either level your wings and the other fighter gets a kill or you become a "rocks kill" by crashing into mother earth as you continue to struggle but get nowhere.

The same scenario happens in business when there isn't an environment for corporate growth. Owners chase employees that only see a dead-end job, trying to motivate them. Without the prospect of growth, your employees will level their wings and give up the fight. Without employees trying, the owner eventually hits the rocks because they can't do it themselves.

Without a desire for company growth, stagnation sets in. Top performers want to challenge themselves by taking on more responsibility. When companies stagnate, the only growth opportunity is when a position becomes available because someone leaves. Since advancement opportunities are few and far between, typically the top performers leave seeking opportunities elsewhere. This leaves the "also-rans", those teammates that are content with their lot. Though usually stable, these are the team members that won't go the extra mile. They aren't innovative or creative and require much closer supervision than the go-getters.

In my experience, corporate stagnation is a result of burnout. Ownership is tired of fighting an uphill battle, and they don't believe it can get any better without a great deal more effort on their part. Typically, this happens in well-established companies. Financially these companies are usually, but not always, barely profitable. They are never working at peak profitability. Owners draw an income, but there is no real source of financial wealth. As top performers leave for greener pastures, it only reinforces the owner's perception that growth can only occur if they spend more time working.

For example, I recall meeting with the owner of an outdoors sporting shop in Duluth, Minnesota. The store had been in business for 30 years, the owner started the business in his young 20's. Originally a bait and tackle shop, they had slowly expanded their product offerings to include hunting and fishing gear. It was like a smaller Bass Pro shop. Their annualized revenue was about $1.2 million. To put this in perspective, according to the website businessknowhow.com, in a 2012 survey only 4% of small businesses, companies with less than 50 employees, generated sales in excess of $1 million. The average net profits in retail is 3.4%. This is the amount left over after buying your inventory and paying for all of your expenses, including a fair salary to the owner. According to this calculation, the owners should have been making about $40K. Because this store was barely breaking even, the owner was only paying himself a modest salary of $31,000 per year. He couldn't afford to pay himself any more than that. His staff wasn't motivated, absenteeism was rampant, and there was high turnover. Unfortunately for his staff, he was content with the status quo. His wife earned a good living and he was either content to be a business owner, regardless of the success of the business, or he didn't believe that he could grow the business or run it better. In the end, it didn't matter what the reason was. He failed to provide an environment of growth, meaning he was the hardest-working employee. He was chasing his own tail trying to motivate his employees, all while keeping his company from becoming a "rocks kill."

In the jet fighter community, we have a saying, "speed is life." This refers to the advantages you have when you are faster than your opponent. A business is either growing or shrinking, so for business "growth is life."

If your company isn't growing, it's dying. Our inherent sense of self-preservation means it is difficult or impossible to lead people to their death. When employees don't have the sense of security that comes from knowing their company is growing and doing well, employees look for a more stable company with better prospects. Most owners want to grow their business, but that isn't the same as having an environment of growth. The mere desire is not sufficient; you need to have an active plan.

Developing Your Active Plan for Growth

Before creating an effective growth strategy, you need to know your target market. You may think your market is anyone who wants to use your services, but really, that isn't true. We all know that some customers are better than others. Likewise, you may think attacking any enemy target is good, but the reality is some targets are better than others. When attacked, some yield disproportionate results. Attacking a ground target from the air while traveling at speeds of 500 mph is not easy. A large bridge over a river doesn't always stand out from 10,000 feet. At those speeds, you can miss it if you come in low to avoid radar and then pop up to altitude. If you don't know what you are looking for, what may appear obvious to the casual observer on the ground can be easily missed. To hit the target, aviators engage in a target study. They review aerial photographs and look for clues that tell them exactly where the target is located. To be successful in business and ensure an environment of corporate growth, you also need your own target study. You need to figure out the clues that increase the probability that new customers will be good customers.

To do this, first you need to know your values. If you haven't done so, now is the time to do the Locked On Values Exercise in Chapter 4. Ask yourself the following questions: "Why are you in the business you are in? What is it that attracts you to the business? How are you personally fulfilled by engaging in the business?" Although you don't need to know all the answers to create an effective environment for growth, it is essential for attracting the right people who share your passion. Whereas the leadership skills discussed in this book will elevate any team, the better your raw material, the better your end results. Having a clear understanding of your values and purpose allows you to hire team members with similar values and who embrace your purpose.

Next, you need to look to your market. You should narrow your niche to laser precision. At first, this may seem counterintuitive. After all, you want as many customers as possible, or do you? Wouldn't you really want more *profitable* customers? To do so, you need to apply the Law of the Vital Few. First observed by Italian economist Vilfredo Pareto, the Law of the Vital Few, also known as the Pareto Principal or the 80/20 rule, postulates that a small number of any group will hold a disproportionate amount of the resources. The approximate split is 20% of a group will have 80% of the resources. In business, typically 80% of the revenue comes from 20% of the customers—these are your spenders. Likewise, 80% of your problems come from a different 20% of your customers—these are your headaches. There may be some overlap between the spenders and headaches.

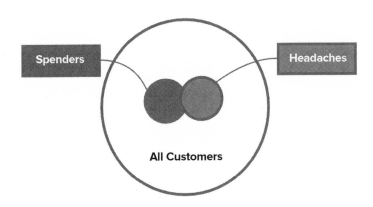

Locked On Target Study Exercise

1. Identify your "Spenders" and "Headaches." It's easy to identify spenders as most accounting software will allow you to run a revenue report by customer. Simply sort it by revenue, count the number of clients, determine how many clients make up 20%, then add up the revenue of the top 20% of your clients. It probably won't be exactly 80%, but it will be a significant amount of your revenue.

2. Identify what your Spenders have in common. It may be industry, the number of employees, their client base, location, revenue, operational problems, types of capital assets, etc. Don't limit your thinking. Conduct a brainstorming session with your sales team where no one critiques an answer. Allow team members to call out uncensored answers and write them down. Once you have exhausted most of the possibilities, it's time to winnow down the list by combining like descriptors. During the process, you may discover that sometimes there are descriptors that depict different parameters, but point to the same information. For example, one of my clients is an IT Managed Services Provider. While going through this process we had "> 10 employees" and "> 10 computers." After some discussion, we realized that some clients had more employees than computers. We ended up tossing out the "> 10 employees" descriptor and ultimately settled on "> 10 computing devices" to account for handheld devices like tablets and phones.

3. Identify your Headaches. Identify the defining characteristics of your Headaches by going through the same exercise you did for the Spenders.

4. Now look at the subset of Spenders who are not Headaches. Review their demographics, then review anything that can be measured like their industry, number of

employees, annual revenue. Then look at their psycho-graphics, their aspirations, attitudes, and other psycholog-ical criteria. Although these are more difficult to define, they will provide great information. Consider what is their motivation, what are they afraid of, and what they hope to gain. Anything that describes "why" they buy is helpful. Here's a hint: if your answer is price-related, you missed the boat. If you have trouble with this, hire a marketing company that uses psychographics as part of their market-ing efforts. They should be able to help you identify your top buyer's motivation. This is your target market.

5. Develop a business strategy around the psychographics and demographics of your top, non-headache Spenders. Market strongly to this group. If done correctly, expect to see some dynamic and very profitable growth.

Without an active plan for growth, you will lose your top team members to your competitors. Expect to be drained of energy and motivation while enduring yet another cycle of talent replace-ment. In contrast, top talent can grow with the company when you have a solid strategy for growth. This allows you to focus on other areas while your top talent do their jobs enthusiastically and well.

2. Clear Job Descriptions

Business owners are not the only ones that run around in circles until they hit the ground. Employees that don't truly understand their responsibilities act in a similar fashion. In the military, to prevent becoming a "rocks kill" during training we establish a "hard deck," typically set at 10,000 feet of altitude. If an aircraft flies below the hard deck, we "knock it off" or stop the fight. The fighter that flew below the hard deck is considered a "rocks kill" and the other fighter victorious. In real combat operations and in training we would brief a "soft deck." Below this altitude completing certain maneuvers would be considered extremely dangerous as you most likely would hit the ground, the true hard deck.

If you've ever worked at a job with poor or no job description, you know how disconcerting this can be. Certainly, for me, as a young man, this lack of a job description cost me my first job as a busboy. Job descriptions tell everyone for what and to whom the position is accountable. In a 2011 study conducted at the University of Washington, researcher Stephen Barbouletos studied the effect of Job Discrepancies on the workplace. Barbouletos defines Job Discrepancies as "…the difference between formal job descriptions and true job expectations.[13] He concluded that "Higher job discrepancy increases stress and tension for all employees in the workplace.[14] I cannot overstate the potential power of an accurate and well-written job description.

A well written job description provides team members with control of their own destiny. They know what is expected of them and, when coupled with a good employee handbook, know the consequences of failure to meet those standards.

A good job description, like any standard company procedure, sets the minimum acceptable standard for job performance. In fighter aviation, this is referred to as "the hard deck."

Locked On Tip

Ask your team members to write their own job descriptions, based on what they actually do. Compare them to your existing descriptions to uncover any job discrepancies. If you don't have existing job descriptions, use these as a starting point.

To create a meaningful job description, you first need to define the position's key accountabilities. In other words, why the job exists. This may seem obvious, but it is not always the case. It is not uncommon for people to be hired to do one thing only to end up doing something completely different. For example, my client hired an office manager just before we started working together. They thought they needed someone who was qualified to manage an office and handle general administrative tasks. I noticed she was doing predominantly bookkeeping and accounting functions—tasks she had no experience with whatsoever. She worked hard to learn the new skills, but the company suffered, as did she. The owners weren't happy with her performance. In turn, she was unhappy because she could never do anything to their satisfaction. After a couple of years, she left to work elsewhere and they needed to find someone new. This time, armed with an accurate job description, they looked for someone with the right behaviors, soft skills, and hard skills needed for the job. The new person is working out very well while completing tasks in half the time with twice the accuracy. Now the owners can focus on growing their business instead of mitigating problems.

LOCKED ON KEY ACCOUNTABILITIES EXERCISE

1. Start creating your job descriptions by gathering the stakeholders for the position. These would be anyone currently doing the job, peers who directly interact with the position, direct reports and direct supervisors. You only need one or two representatives from each category.

2. Identify who the customers are for the position. Customers can be internal staff, external vendors, or external buyers. For example, an Accounts Payable Clerk's customers may be the Controller (internal staff), Production Manager (internal staff), and suppliers (external vendor). A Customer Service Rep's customers may be the Sales Department (internal staff), Shipping Department (internal staff), and the end user (external buyer).

3. List everything the job holder does for each customer. The A/P Clerk's statements may read something like:
   - Confirm vendor invoices against PO's and packing slips
   - Enter invoice into accounting system for payment
   - Contact vendors to clear up invoicing discrepancies
   - Develop list of payables for Controller approval
   - Generate A/P aging report
   - Inform Production Manager of any problems with vendors
   - Make sure vendors receive payment on or before due date
   - Download all company credit card transactions daily
4. Create 25-30 statements describing the responsibilities of each position.
5. Group the statements into like responsibilities. In our example above you might group:
   - "Confirm vendor invoices against PO's and packing slips" with
   - "Enter invoice into accounting system for payment" and
   - "Contact vendors to clear up invoicing discrepancies."
   Typically, you will end up with four or five groups of like responsibilities.
6. Write an accountability statement for each grouping. The format of the statement should read "Accountable to _____ to/for _____." In our previous example, it might read: "Accountable to the controller to confirm all vendor invoices for accuracy, clearing up any discrepancies with the vendors, and entering the bill into the accounting system." Each position should have four or five statements like this.

These are your key accountability statements. They don't represent everything, but describe the vast majority of the work since this is why the job exists in the first place.

Job descriptions also typically include:

- who the person reports to,
- whether the job is full-time, part-time, seasonal, or temporary,
- education requirements (if any),
- skills requirements (if any), and
- physical requirements such as "must be able to stand for four hours without sitting" or "must be able to lift 20 lbs. repetitively."

Since employment laws differ from state to state, it is best to consult with an HR professional or employment lawyer for advice. From a leadership perspective, the more accurate information you provide a team member, the better they can self-regulate. An inaccurate job description is a written lie. It damages your credibility and weakens your integrity. Make sure your job descriptions are accurate and keep them up-to-date.

3. Simple Metrics

War movies show the power of metrics. Painted on the side of each aircraft is a small symbol representing the number of enemy planes and boats destroyed. In combat, metrics are simple.

- For sailors and airmen, the metric is enemy assets destroyed;
- For soldiers or marines, area under control, and
- Merchant marines, metric tons delivered.

When you get the metrics right, jobs become easier. Proper metrics provide us with laser-like focus on what is important. We focus on the unimportant when we have the wrong metric. Nowhere was this more obvious than during our struggles in Vietnam.

Robert McNamara was the Secretary of Defense under JFK. During World War II McNamara was part of an elite Pentagon team called Statistical Controls, utilizing data analysis to streamline logistics and quantify the war effort. After the war, he was hired to help turn around the Ford Motor Company. His penchant for numbers eventually resulted in his promotion to President before JFK asked him to serve as the Secretary of Defense.

McNamara took his love of numbers and applied them to the entire Department of Defense. Although there were many positive results, success in Vietnam was not one of them. The Vietnam strategy was to break the will of the North Vietnamese. Senior military leadership believed if they could kill more North Vietnamese soldiers than could be replaced, they could achieve their strategic goal. The Defense Department settled on "body count" as the metric to measure the effectiveness of their tactics. This is a prime example of a flawed metric. Officers were judged based on their ability to deliver body count so they were included in each after-action report. These counts were often inaccurate. The North Vietnamese and Viet Cong would care for their dead, just like we did. They removed them from the battlefield to be properly interred. Because accurate body counts were impossible to achieve, the numbers were almost always exaggerated.

As a result of these flawed metrics, the senior military leaders in Vietnam believed we were making headway. They believed we were closing in on the "tipping point," when there weren't enough men of fighting age to replace the NVA soldiers killed. By relying on body count as a metric, they weren't able to see the big picture and adjust their strategy. Meanwhile, the North Vietnamese measured success by the size of the geographic area in South Vietnam under their control. If your goal is to take control of a country, this is a much more accurate metric and one easier to measure.

Creating metrics may seem simple, but it is not easy. There are multiple landmines hidden beneath the surface. Like landmines, they can be detected with a little bit of diligence.

Accurately Measure Metrics

The first landmine exploded under me when in 1999, I became the VP of Operations for a telecommunications company. The owner viewed the operations department as a profit center. He wanted us to increase revenue because, by his calculations, the department was losing money. The problem was as a department, we had no control over income.

The company generated revenue from four sources: new equipment sales; relocating existing equipment when a client moved their offices; Moves, Adds and Changes (MACs) to an existing system within the same building; and, service calls— repairing equipment that was not functioning properly. Of these four revenue sources, operations handled MACs and service calls. Over 80% of the company's revenue was generated by the sales department, but 75% of the direct labor cost was in operations. This was a problem as the operations department could only be a profit center by moving revenue over from the sales department.

The company created a bonus plan for me. The result was a bonus structure so convoluted and difficult to understand that I had no idea how to earn my bonus. To make matters worse, when I asked the owner about the bonus plan, he couldn't explain it to me. He was clear, however, that his intention was for me to drive revenue in the operations department.

There were two problems with this bonus. The first is obvious. My bonus was based on something I had little to no control over. MACs were a result of our client's internal changes and service calls happened when equipment needed repair. No amount of calling or marketing would result in increasing MACs and nothing short of sabotage would increase service calls. Loss to competitors wasn't an issue as our customers were locked into using us. I could have attempted to market to new customers but that was a sales function and the sales department was already doing that.

The second problem with the bonus was if we charged our actual cost for the labor, we wouldn't have made any money on the installations and they took up much of our time. We couldn't move the cost of the technicians to the sales department because I needed to allot for the time of the customer service reps. In other words, there was no accurate way to determine our cost of installation and charge the sales department. The accountant put a guesstimate on our cost, but it was far from accurate.

The result? I ignored the bonus and the company never achieved their goal of having the operations department run as a profit center. Instead of creating a win-win scenario where the company got what it wanted, and I got more money, they created a lose–lose scenario where we each got neither. This leads to the next requirement of good metrics—they must incent the right behavior(s).

Beware of Positive, Disastrous Results

Besides accurate metrics, you have to incent the right behavior.

In 2009, I was the President of a kitchen and bath remodeling company. The owner was a self-professed entrepreneur who claimed he knew how to start companies but not grow them past a certain size. The compensation package included a bonus based on increased sales revenue. Since the owner wanted to grow the business, he thought this was the right metric. I initially argued he needed to increase profits, but he rejected that idea. While sales grew, it took about six months before I received accurate financials. That's when I discovered that the problem wasn't our sales volume. The increase in sales actually accelerated our losses due to more production waste. I met with the owner and pointed out the problem. I argued, once again, that we needed to increase our profits. He insisted that growing sales would solve the problem. The result was predictable.

The metric I was given, sales, increased with the disastrous effect of accelerating our losses. Ultimately the company filed for bankruptcy and a lot of people were hurt. In this case, there was no ill intent as the owner didn't think about the unintended negative consequences of his actions. However, that isn't always the case. Sometimes people just game the system.

I got my first sales job when I was 21. I was hired as an account representative for a national company that made and sold industrial cleaning chemicals. I struggled as it was a 100% commission job with a small draw. After training, I started hitting my territory. I was far from successful. I didn't know how to ask good, open-ended questions to uncover needs and as a result, I wasn't selling very much. To "help me" my sales manager came with me on some sales calls. We pulled up to a business and he said, "They've bought from us in the past so they should be easy, but whatever you do, don't mention my name at all." I thought that was strange. Later on, I found out in the past they had been his big account. He had gained their trust so he would take inventory for them and then tell them what they needed. The customer would order it based on his recommendation. This went on for some time until one day, the customer noticed he was overstocked on just about everything. My sales manager made his bonus each month because of this account. If he was having a slow month, he would pretend they were low on a product and have the customer order it. When I showed up, my sales manager was persona non grata and the customer used a competitor's product.

This scenario happens time and time again in public companies. Executives receive stock options as bonuses. Their incentive is to drive the stock price higher. On the surface, this seems like a win-win. However, all too often senior executives manipulate stock prices for personal gain but to the long-term detriment of the company.

This is what I refer to as positive disastrous results. Whenever somebody achieves their number but only they benefit and nobody else, it's the quintessential win-lose. Positive disastrous results can occur naturally or intentionally.

Using multiple, competing metrics can solve this problem. Lean manufacturing practices use this concept exceptionally well. A manufacturing facility that uses lean processes prominently displays an SQDC board. Usually this is a dry erase board with the daily metrics of four competing parameters: safety, quality, delivery, and cost. Lean practitioners know you need to measure all of these parameters.

If you only measure "cost," quality suffers when you use inexpensive materials that fail. This results in higher returns costing the company time, money, and reputation. If "delivery" is the only concern, workers may work too fast causing more accidents which impacts "safety." Should you only measure "quality," production times may suffer or it ends up costing too much. Once again wasting time, money, and reputation. Similarly, a singular focus on "safety" to the exclusion of all else could result in slow, costly processes.

You can apply this principle to other areas as well. For example, instead of just focusing on revenue for salespeople, why not include accuracy of order, charge-backs and profitability? This way, salespeople are incented not to sell something a customer doesn't need, omit something they do need, as well as making sure the product sells for a profit.

The right metrics drive behaviors and, like good job descriptions, puts the team member in control of their own destiny. Most people want to do well. Since employment represents our ability to provide food and shelter to ourselves and our family, our "Need" is to keep our job and advance in our career where possible. Having a target number to hit, in an area that we control, provides us with that ability.

In short, there is a positive return to the company when you have simple metrics that measure team members' activities that they control.

DEVELOPING METRICS EXERCISE

1. **Determine your primary metric.** Look at your key accountabilities for each job. What can you objectively measure to see how the employee is performing? Examples include:
   a. Operations – production level, delivery schedule, inventory
   b. Accounting – receivables, payables
   c. Purchasing – inventory levels
   d. Marketing – impressions, leads, conversions
   e. Salesperson – revenue, cold calls made, proposals delivered

   A note on sales: Sales can be measured by volume, activity or a combination of the two.

2. **Determine your secondary metric(s).** What additional parameters do you need to ensure a triple win? Examples include:
   a. Operations – delivery, WIP (work in process), returns, labor cost
   b. Accounting – days to pay, accuracy
   c. Purchasing – inventory turns, shrinkage
   d. Marketing – sales appointments, average sale, bounce rate
   e. Salesperson – gross profit, charge-backs, reorders, customer turnover, closing rate

3. **Assign a value to each metric.**
4. **Create a tracking system for your metrics.**

5. **By job description, determine your review frequency.** Some metrics, like those for manufacturing, may need daily reviews. Others may require weekly or monthly reviews. As a general rule, the more frequently you review a metric, the easier issues are to correct before becoming a major problem. However, some processes may take longer than others. In sales, for example, the general rule is the greater the cost, the longer the sale cycle. Someone selling multifunction printers will have a shorter sales cycle than someone selling airliners. If you are using revenue as a primary metric, measuring monthly sales for the printers and annual sales for the airliners makes the most sense. Activity-based metrics for large ticket sales are advised since these can then be measured weekly, or even daily.

6. **Develop a review/correction process.** See the Quality Board (Q-Board) discussion in Chapter 9.

4. Formalized Training

The loudspeaker comes to life and a whistle emanates from it modulating from a sustained low pitch to a higher pitch, a pattern familiar to me from all the WWII movies I watched growing up. It is the sound of a Bosun's Pipe, and this is the first time hearing it in person, in a real-life situation. An announcement follows the whistle, "Underway, shift colors." The deck starts to throb under my feet as the four, powerful, diesel turbine engines throttle up and thrust us away from the pier. You wouldn't think you could feel movement when you are on a ship weighing over 60,000 tons moving at less than five knots, but you can. We're getting underway for "Refresher Training" or "REFTRA" (pronounced Ref-Tray) as it's known in Naval jargon. I am a nugget RIO (Radar Intercept Officer). We fly in the back seats of the F-14 Tomcat, think Goose, Anthony Edward's character from the movie *Top Gun*. As this is my first time at sea, I'm a little nervous, although I would never admit that to anyone should they ask. After all, fighter pilots need to keep cool at all times. I take all this in subconsciously as I carefully peruse the message board while sitting in our ready room onboard the U.S.S. Independence. The nervousness I feel intensifies, perhaps it is all the coffee I've had. I walked onboard at 0300, or 3 am for all you civilians, and tried to sleep in my stateroom but I was too excited for sleep. So, I dressed in my wash khakis and went to the ready room where the perpetual pot of coffee lives. It is now 0900, 9 am, and I'm thinking four cups of Joe might have been overdoing it a bit. With the excitement and nerves of my first time at sea, I'm starting to feel a little light-headed, and reading isn't helping. I glance up from the message board and look at the Platt Cameras, the shipboard closed-circuit TV system. There are cameras on the flight deck and the superstructure and in every space, (that's what we sailors call a room), on the ship there are TV's. One of the channels gives us access to the cameras. We can watch flight operations or other shipboard evolutions. Now, they're focused on the port side, and I can see we're underway. Like a grand revelation it hits me; the sensations I've been feeling are not nerves or coffee, it's the motion of the ocean. In this case, the San Diego Bay. My stomach immediately calms down after realizing this, although my excitement remains high.

REFTRA will be my first opportunity to catapult off the flight deck. Although I have been in the Navy for three years and have logged over 200 hours in various aircraft, at this point, I had never taken off from, nor trapped on (landed pn) an aircraft carrier. This singular event is a rite of passage for carrier-based Naval Aviators, the Navy's official name for its pilots, and Naval Flight Officers (NFO), those of us who don't control the flying of the aircraft but are responsible for its tactical systems, like me. Pilots have to trap to earn their wings but NFO's like me don't usually get to trap until we've completed training and have joined our first fleet squadron. I'm scheduled to fly with the skipper later that day, once we clear San Diego Bay and are out to sea in the designated "Military Operating Area" off the coast of southern California.

Several hours later, I step onto the flight deck. To the untrained eye, the flight deck of an aircraft carrier during flight operations appears to be nothing more than a cacophony of color and sound. Flight deck personnel wearing long-sleeved turtleneck jerseys in a multitude of colors blend with the noise of jet engines turning, radios blaring, and occasional announcements over the 5MC, the flight deck's loud speaker system. During Officer Candidate School, we learned about the various colored jerseys and what they meant, but at this point I'm a little overwhelmed. Although I've been thoroughly briefed on the dangers of the flight deck during air operations, the reality of the frenetic activity defies logic.

Walking in my pilot's wake to keep out of trouble, I find my aircraft, perform my preflight inspection and strap into the rear cockpit of an F-14A Tomcat. Strapping into the front is our Executive Officer or XO, Commander Charles "Heater" Heatley. Heater is famous for publishing a coffee table photo essay book on Naval Aviation entitled The Cutting Edge. He was also an extra in the famous Officer's Club scene in Top Gun when Maverick and Goose serenade "Charlie," Kelly McGillis' character, with The Righteous Brothers' "You've Lost That Lovin' Feelin'." Today, however, Heater is all business. He, like all pilots, has to Carrier Qualify (CQ) once again. In spite of having over 1,000 "traps," Heater must prove he is still up to the task. Landing on the deck of an aircraft carrier is serious business. It is the most stressful evolution any pilot can experience. A study done during the Vietnam War determined that a pilot was under more stress during carrier landings than during actual combat.[15] To qualify, pilots must have 10-day and 6-night landings. If a pilot goes for more than 1 week without a night landing, they have to requalify.

There is no evolution more closely monitored than carrier landings. Each one is graded. The highest grade a pilot aspires to is an "OK" landing, followed by a "fair," a "no grade," and a "cut pass." Each landing grade for each pilot is prominently displayed on a board, known as the "Greenie Board" in the squadron's ready room. Picture a matrix with the pilot's names at the left of each column and a grade for each landing indicated in columns across. Grades are indicated by color, green for OK, yellow for fair or no grade, and brown, disparagingly referred to as a turd, for cut passes. The best pilots have a string of greens, thus the name Greenie Board. The first thing any aircrew does upon entering any ready room is check out the "Greenie Board" to see who the good pilots are and who is struggling. Senior pilots, such as "Heater," are always at or near the top of the Greenie Board due to their years of experience, but no one takes it lightly.

Back in our aircraft, we are ready for engine start. After giving the "all clear" signal, I bring down the canopy. Heater starts the left engine, then the right. With both engines on line, we each go through our post start-up checklists. I power up the radar, communications, and weapon systems. Up until this point, I'm following procedures that I had performed countless times during land-based training operations. However, when the chocks are removed from the wheels, and the yellow-shirted aircraft handler signals us to pull forward, everything changes.

During shore-based operations I have little to do during this part of the evolution, but on board a carrier it is all different. I don't need to call "Ground Control" for taxi clearance, instead, I need to find the "weight board" and "roger" our weight. The steam pressure in the catapult has to be set based on the aircraft takeoff weight. Too much and it can damage the aircraft. Too little and the aircraft won't achieve flying speed at the end of the stroke. What we call a "cold cat," resulting in one of two scenarios, neither good. The best outcome is the Navy loses a $40M fighter and Heater and I take an unplanned swim. The worst scenario is a total loss of aircraft and crew. I find the green shirt holding the weight board and check it against our dry weight plus fuel load. Even though this information has been passed from our maintenance chief to the catapult crew, I am the ultimate check. The numbers add up and I give the thumbs up. While this is going on, Heater is expertly maneuvering our aircraft into position behind the jet blast deflector, or JBD, on Cat 2, the left catapult on the bow of the Indy.

We're next in line. An F/A-18 Hornet takes off in front of us. The nose of our aircraft is scant feet away from his exhaust, but the steel JBD protects us. I'm surprised that we feel the buffeting as our aircraft rocks when the Hornet lights up his afterburners. Then he shoots into the sky as he's catapulted off the flight deck. Immediately, the JBD lowers as the Aircraft Director, using nothing but hand signals, directs Heater forward to line up our aircraft onto the catapult. While taxiing forward to engage the tow bar into the shuttle that will propel us down the flight deck, Heater sweeps the wings forward from the stowed, carrier position to the forward position for takeoff. Simultaneously, the safety checks are performed by the final checkers, experienced maintenance crews from my squadron. Although our aircraft has been looked at by the maintenance Chief, our Plane Captain, Heater, and me, the final checkers have the last say. Two of them approach the aircraft and walk down its length, one on either side. They are looking for anything out of the ordinary. One wrong step and they can easily get sucked down the maws of our massive engine intakes to be chewed up and spit out like so much beef into a meat grinder. When everything is good, they will each give and hold thumbs up indicating they see no reason not to launch. If they see something amiss, they can fail the launch.

Meanwhile, Heater is going through his final checks under the direction of the Catapult Officer. He is directed to manipulate all of the control surfaces to ensure operations. He gets the signal to deploy the spoilers to confirm they are working. This is one of the last go/no-go checks. The F-14 was designed without ailerons, the traditional control surface used to make an airplane roll on its longitudinal axis. During low-speed flight regiments, such as takeoffs and landings, spoilers provide this function. Failure of the spoilers to deploy will scrub the launch. I'm watching everything with wide eyes, excited about the upcoming cat shot, eagerly anticipating the acceleration to over 170 mph in under two seconds. My reverie is broken by Heater angrily speaking to me on the intercom, "Check the spoiler circuit breaker!" Apparently, we failed the spoilers check.

The circuit breaker in question is located at the top of the circuit breaker panel on the left aft bulkhead, next to my seat. You can't easily see it while strapped in, you just have to feel it with your hand. During land-based operations this circuit breaker remains depressed or "on" but during carrier operations the breaker is pulled to prevent the spoilers from deploying when power is put on the aircraft with the wings swept back for carrier storage. When pulled, the breaker is popped out and stands out above all the other breakers. I flail around "looking" for the errant breaker with my gloved hands. I don't feel anything extended above the others and tell Heater that it is in. He tries the spoilers again and they don't work.

We're just about to scrub the launch when I find the recalcitrant breaker and it is, in fact, popped. I instantly realize that I misspoke when I told Heater it was in. Not wanting to call attention to my ignorance, I push it in and tell Heater, "I just cycled the breaker, try it again." Heater signals for one more check, the spoilers deploy and we get the thumbs up. Heater says "good job RP" (my call sign), the catapult officer signals for tension. The catapult shuttle inches forward to engage the holdback bar that will restrain our aircraft until the catapult launch is initiated. He then signals Heater to go to full power by extending his middle and index finger as if he is holding a cigarette, waiving them back and forth. Heater pushes the throttles forward up to the afterburner detents and our Tomcat strains to leap off the deck as our engines pump out over 30,000 lbs. of thrust. Having never catapulted from the deck of a carrier before, I briefly wonder if

I will even recognize a cold cat shot and pull the ejection handle in time, then I consign my fate to the furies. The Catapult Officer extends his hand over his head, all five fingers splayed, indicating we are to go to full afterburner. Twin columns of fire shoot out of exhaust nozzles as Heater pushes the throttle through the afterburner detents, dumping raw fuel into our exhaust and increasing the thrust to over 33,000 lbs.

Heater checks his flight controls one more time, then salutes the Cat Officer signaling he is ready for takeoff. The Cat Officer returns the salute, looks at the final checkers one more time, thumbs up all around, he crouches, touches the deck and points towards the bow. On the side of the flight deck, a sailor, whose hands have been raised above his head since we went into tension to prevent a premature launch touches a button with his right hand. I am violently and emphatically thrust into my seat, my body weighing over four times its normal weight, as the pent-up steam is released and our 30 tons of aircraft is accelerated to speeds in excess of 170 mph. Two seconds later, I experience an apparent, split-second of weightlessness as the catapult reaches the end of its stroke and our aircraft is thrust into the sky at 170 mph.

"Gear up, flaps up," Heater tells me on the intercom as we climb to 500 feet. Normally we would head out until we depart the carrier's air control zone and proceed on mission, but not today. Today we fly upwind at 600 feet looking for the aircraft that departed before ours. Once spotted, we turn downwind behind him, paralleling the carrier's path, heading aft to a position behind him so we can set up for our landing. Our goal is to land exactly 45 seconds after he does.

Today's mission is twofold. First getting Heater, and the other pilots in the Airwing, re-qualified for carrier operations, second is to give the flight deck crew practice at launching and recovering aircraft. An aircraft carrier has to sail a straight line during recovery operations. This makes them predictable and being predictable in combat is asking for trouble. The faster an airwing can recover from flight operations, that's what we call the landing evolution, recovery, the sooner the Captain of the ship can start maneuvering. Somewhere it was determined that 45 seconds is the optimum amount of time between planes landing. This allows the arresting gear crew to reset the cable between aircraft while the pilot of the just-landed aircraft maneuvers out of the landing area, making room for the following pilot.

"Hook down," I hear over the intercom system as Heater deploys the arresting hook. Although there are no flight controls in the rear cockpit of an F-14, Heater walks me through the procedures. There are many good reasons for this. Not the least of which is that at some point in my future I will be the experienced crew member flying with a new pilot, affectionately referred to as a nugget. I need to be able to confirm they are doing everything right. Also, a pilot may be injured in combat or the aircraft damaged. Under these circumstances a pilot could get overwhelmed and I need to be able to back them up. I can't fly the aircraft but that doesn't mean I can't take some of the load of off the pilot. After all, my life may depend on it.

Heater continues, "Flaps" I hear as we slow to 150 knots followed by "3-down and green." Heater's confirming that all three of our wheels are down and the indicator lights are all showing green. We are now abeam of the carrier, about 1.5 miles away, flying in the opposite direction of the ship's direction of travel. As we pass the stern, Heater pulls a little power, decreasing the throttle to begin our descent while he simultaneously starts a gentle left-hand turn. We are turning onto the base leg of our landing pattern, the precursor to our final approach, the most dangerous part of the landing. The geometry caused by the F-14's large aircraft body and the position of our engine inlets mean it is very easy to block the airflow to one of our engines and cause it to stall. If this occurs at altitude with sufficient airspeed, it can result in an unrecoverable flat spin. During landing operations, your aircraft simply flops over and hits the water. You have scant seconds to react and eject. Since the pilot is so busy flying, the responsibility for ejecting would be solely mine.

We continue to descend while turning, crossing the ship's wake at approximately 350 feet above sea level. Heater starts to level his wings, rolling out lined up with the angle deck. "Ball," he says on the intercom, telling me he sees the optical landing system. Unlike the movies, this is not transmitted over the radio during normal daytime recovery operations. We don't want to give our position away with errant radio signals. Our aircraft rolls slightly right as Heater corrects our lineup to account for the ship's movement.

I lock my seat harness and brace myself on a handle situated at the top of my radar screen designed for this purpose. Fifteen seconds later we crash into the flight deck at a rate of 600 feet per second, landing struts compressing with forces that would destroy the landing gear of shore-based aircraft. Heater pushes the throttles to full power in case we don't catch a wire and "bolter" off the flight deck. Going to full power will ensure we have enough speed to fly away safely. I'm flung violently forward, my seat's safety harness tightens to keep me from smashing into the instrument console as the arresting hook engages the cross-deck cable and our 60,000 lb. aircraft decelerates from 150 mph to a dead stop in two seconds. Although my seat harness is locked, I'm glad I listened to the experienced RIOs and braced myself. No sooner do we stop then I see an Aircraft Director signal hook up and we start taxiing to the forward catapult. We will repeat this process three more times, then go back and get two landings that night.

The Navy, and military in general, spends a huge amount of time training. This makes sense. War is a complicated endeavor. Tens of thousands of personnel perform complex tasks in a fluid and uncontrolled environment where someone opposes your every move. Training is required for any military to be effective. The growth of the Roman and British empires is directly attributed to the training of their respective armies. Military training is extremely comprehensive and no part of a member's life is over-looked. In boot camp, trainees are taught how to dress, walk, talk, and even eat. As you advance in the military, your training continues. Enlisted personnel are provided skill-specific training for their job. Once enlisted reach a senior rank, they go through non-commissioned officer training and possibly War College. Likewise, Officers go through an analogous series of training rarely found in any civilian organization. A Naval Aviator or Air Force pilot may not see a front-line squadron for three years. Once they reach their first squadron, training continues. This is just one example. Military missions can be widely varied and incorporate national security, humanitarian, diplomatic, power projection, law enforcement, governance, and a host of other objectives. All require differing skill sets, and therefore, different training requirements.

Training in Business

Business is rarely as complex as the military, but that doesn't mean training is less important. All too often, training is an afterthought, especially in small businesses where it has the greatest impact. Imagine running a small business selling shoes over the internet. If you have one single customer service representative, the impact this individual has on your company's reputation is incalculable. They are the single point of contact between you and your customers. Despite their importance, most of the time we do little or no training. If we do provide training, it is almost always tribal. More on that in a little bit.

We typically rely on experience. We hire someone with a customer service background who seems pleasant and has a good recommendation from a past employer. If they are a good fit, you're lucky. If your company grows and you hire a second customer service representative, will callers get the same experience? Most likely not if you don't have a formal training program. Ultimately, this dilutes your brand and makes growth a challenge. I've seen small companies struggling to grow for years because they don't provide training. They may get lucky and hire someone who is naturally talented or already has sufficient training from a previous employer. As a result, the company surges forward only to slide backwards because the talent leaves. Similarly, bad hires that are not trained suck up valuable resources. Instead of focusing on growth, management deals with incompetence.

By contrast, let's look at a larger company such as Zappos. In 2014, Zappos had over 600 members on their Customer Loyalty Team. These customer service representatives handle approximately 7,500 customer contacts per day by chat session, email, or phone call. One poorly trained customer service rep at Zappos will statistically have a minimal impact, handling less than 1% of all contacts. Yet Zappos created an entire department, Zappos University, to provide both mandatory and elective training for its team members. As a result, Zappos was one of Fortune's top 100 places to work for seven years in a row (2008-2015).

Zappos' focus on customer service stems from their belief that customer retention is the best form of marketing. In a 2014 interview with Forbes,[16] Zappos CEO Tony Hsieh said:

> "Our business is based on repeat customers and word of mouth. There's a lot of value in building up our brand name and what it stands for. We view the money that we spend on customer service as marketing money that improves our brand."

However, there is another reason to focus on training. Training leverages our deep-seated need for reciprocity. Cultural anthropologists theorize that reciprocity developed as a survival trait in early humans. Reciprocity creates synergy allowing individuals to leverage their strengths for the good of all and, by extension, helping to ensure personal survival because others would be inclined to help you because you helped them in the past. A less skilled hunter may dress a kill or prepare the meal for the more skilled hunter. That way, the skilled hunter could recuperate faster and hunt more. A selfish hunter would not be as successful in this environment. When a company invests time and money to train employees it triggers a strong desire to reciprocate and perform well.

Training also creates a sense of security. When trained, employees realize the company is looking for a return on investment. They implicitly understand they will not be let go needlessly. This creates a sense of security and satisfies Maslow's second need.

Zappos knows the value of training. All new Zappos employees, regardless of position, take a 4 week training course. New employees are trained on Zappos' 10 values and how to apply them, Zappos culture, as well as business processes. All Zappos employees, regardless of their ultimate position, spend 40-hours taking calls from customers. Besides emphasizing the importance of customers, this training allows any employee to act as a backup crew during their busy high volume seasons.

Zappos training and culture is so effective, they created a department called Zappos Insights, to assist other companies in emulating it. But what about attrition and job security? Does all this training really help? According to Christa Foley, Senior Director of Brand Vision & Culture | Head of Talent Acquisition, Zappos' call center only experiences an approximate 14% turnover compared to 100% for other call centers in Las Vegas. That's huge! How much of that is attributed to their training? Well, employee turnover is down from about 55% before the creation of Zappos University.

Your company will benefit from formal training in three distinct ways:

1. Retention of talent. Turnover is exceedingly expensive. Besides the hard costs associated with recruitment and training, there is loss of productivity and tribal knowledge. No matter how well documented your procedures, long-time employees retain knowledge that can never be truly documented. Having long-term motivated employees makes your organization more productive.

2. Better problem solvers. New employees can be more productive and creative in their problem solving abilities when they are trained properly. Knowing that we *know* how to do our job allows us to relax and simply do it. Sports psychologists will tell you that the key to executing a skill at a high level is knowing it well enough that we can do it in our sleep. This allows our conscious mind to disengage and perform the task unconsciously. This is often referred to as "unconscious competence."

Unconscious competence happens when the skill or knowledge is so ingrained it requires no thought. You experience this every time you drive home from work and don't remember the drive. The skill is a habit. Habits reside in our brain in a structure known as the basal ganglia. Neurologists believe conscious thought and processing takes place in our Prefrontal Cortex. When a skill becomes a habit, we free up our Prefrontal Cortex. This allows us to think about other things while performing routine tasks. It is one of the reasons people tend to be more creative in the shower. The act of washing is a habit and requires little or no conscious thought. Research shows the less engaged our Prefrontal Cortex the more creative we become.

When we train our employees, we accelerate the formation of habits which allow them to become more creative. Creative employees help innovate and innovation allows your company to grow. It's the perfect synergistic cocktail.

3. Easier to hold people accountable. As you will see in Chapter 9, holding people accountable actually builds esteem while not holding them accountable, destroys it. When you have formal training, your team members lose the "I didn't know" excuse. Since your training will be formal and syllabus-based, you will cover everything they need to know. You might miss something at first, that's where the Q-Board, which serves as your QC check, comes into play.

Most owners think only of training on the technical skills; this is a mistake. You should have training for every evolution in your company. From what is done by the first person to get there to what is required of the last person to leave, and everything in between. Each of these evolutions should have a written procedure. The training for each evolution should include the hard skills, such as how to use software, tools, and equipment; soft skills like customer service, effective communications, conflict resolution, dealing with change, etc.; your company's procedures, values and purpose.

All procedures need to be trained and then reviewed for compliance. Without compliance, it becomes exponentially more difficult to effectively hold someone accountable to the procedures. I once had a prospective client complain that his company needed to be more nimble. He felt having standard procedures would make them less flexible. Nothing could be farther from the truth.

Few things are more dynamic than combat, yet we have standard procedures. That's because it's easier to improvise by saying execute plan "A" with the following change than it is to make up a new procedure every time. In this case, the person already knows plan "A" so they only have to concentrate on the changes in the plan yielding better and more consistent results.

Business is no different. In reality, 80% or more of your operations fall within a limited, definable norm (there's the Llaw of the Vital few again). Write procedures for these situations. Then look at the remaining 20%. Chances are another 80% of the remaining 20% (that's 16% of the total operations) are a predictable and definable deviation. Incorporate these exceptions into your standard procedures. With these procedures in place you only need to deviate about 4% of the time. Now you only have to identify where you need to deviate from the standard. Adaptation is quicker and you can still manage predictable results. From a leadership perspective, this greatly reduces the stress on your team and sets them up for success.

Creating Training

Every discipline can be broken down into basics, intermediate, and advanced skills. Basics are the individual skills that, by themselves, don't really allow you to do much. They are the constituent parts of intermediate skills.

Let's consider the discipline of reading and writing. The basics are knowing the alphabet and the sounds the individual letters make, knowing how to write the letters of the alphabet, how to combine the letters into simple words, knowing the meanings of words, and simple sentence structure. When you combine these basics skills, you then know how to write at a rudimentary level. For example, "See Jack run." Once you have the basics, you learn more advanced, but still somewhat simplistic skills. We expand our vocabulary from simple words to more complex and nuanced ones and form more advanced sentences. We combine these into paragraphs or other basic writings. Finally, we learn complicated structure for reports, stories, and journalistic or scientific purposes.

Your business is no different. Someone starting in your industry, regardless of their position, needs to learn some rudimentary skills first. Even if they come with the skills, they need to know how *YOU* do them. Whether it's answering the phone or loading paper in a large format printer, no two businesses do everything the exact same way. From accounting to making furniture, there are many "right ways" to do something. You need to define yours by starting with the basics. Provide training to ensure you are delivering the same product, every time, regardless of who is doing the work.

Make sure you have written procedures for the basis of training. In case your procedures are not written down, the following section will show you how to create them. Once you have them, you need to ensure everyone is following them and no one deviates.

Locked On Tip

You need a procedure to change procedures. Don't leave this to chance. Have a way for team members to suggest a change, then test the change. If it is better, promulgate it, and train everyone on the new procedure.

Developing Procedures

1. Identify the procedures you need by major functional area. I recommend following the customer acquisition path from marketing through fulfillment. Then add in the administrative functions necessary to support the sales and operational efforts. This minimizes the chance of missing a critical area. Finally, look at any other areas that you may need. This includes plant & site maintenance and Human Resource functions. The following are typical functional areas that need procedures:
   a. Marketing
   b. Sales
   c. Customer Service
   d. Operations
   e. Research & Development
   f. General Administration
   g. Accounting
   h. Human Resources/Payroll
2. Identify the sub-functions within each major functional area. Customer Service will be different for each company, even within the same industry. Fulfillment may be part of operations in one company and customer service in another. Some companies may have customer service as a sub-routine of Sales or Operations. Purchasing may come

under accounting or it may be an operations function in your organization. There is no *one* right way. When completed, every function you perform should be represented.

3. Create charts for the flow of information and materials through each sub-function (like the one below). These should be 10,000 foot functions. The flow chart starts with either the sub-function that initiates the procedure or a handoff from another major functional area. For example, marketing's sub-functions may include:
   a. Identify marketing message
   b. Transmit marketing message
   c. Receive request for info from prospect
   d. Handoff inquiry to sales
   e. Evaluate marketing effectiveness

The marketing flowchart may look like this:

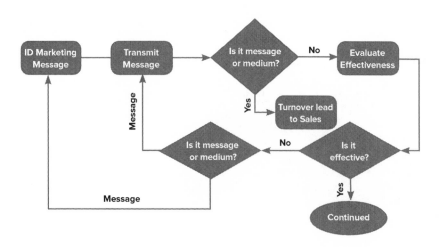

4. Once your flowcharts are created, for each sub-function create a procedure that delineates what needs to be done, who needs to do it, when it needs to be done, how to do it, and why it supports your mission and core values. If the "how" entails using software, that should be in an

Appendix. This way, if you change your software, you only have to modify the Appendix.

If the "how" involves filling out a form, have a sample of the form with a letter in each field that requires information. On the back of the form, list the letter and put in where to obtain the desired information.

Be extremely detailed-oriented, nothing should be left to chance. I usually include minutia such as:

- What to say when answering the phone
- What to say before ending a phone call
- What to do after parking and before going to see the customer
- How to greet the customer at their home and business
- What to say just before leaving a customer's home or office
- Where and when to use the bathroom
- How to leave a customer's bathroom if you have to use it

The more detailed you are in your procedures, the better the end result and the more consistent your customer's experience will be.

Create Your Training Manual

After creating your flow chart and procedures, you need a training manual for each position. Simply take your procedures and arrange them in the order you want a new employee to learn them.

1. Start with the flow charts. One of the top reasons employees leave is they don't understand how they are contributing. I have found that when people understand how their

actions affect others, they tend to make better decisions. The flow chart provides the big picture.

2. Place the procedures in the order of work flow. Start with the most basic or most commonly performed duties. For example, if you are writing the training manual for a dispatcher, you might start with:
   - How to answer the phone, then
   - What to say on the phone, followed by
   - How to triage the service call
   - How to schedule a service call, and finally
   - How to end a call

3. Once you have your procedures, test to see if your new team member knows how to do the procedure. Do this by creating a real-life scenario and see how the trainee handles it. Do they answer the phone right, correctly fill out required forms (digital or physical), and do they manage the software or equipment properly? I typically set up a dummy company and contacts in my CRM, PSA or other software, so trainees can use a "live" system without harm to your active database. Create quizzes for each learning point and a comprehensive exam at the end.

4. Develop answer keys for your quizzes and comprehensive exam. This will provide you with an objective view of their progress and minimize subjective grading. You want your trainees to take their time and learn. You or your training director don't need to spend a great deal of time grading the quizzes and exams.

5. Create a separate training manual for each position.

6. Create a company history training. Every member of your team should know how and why your company started. In addition, you want to cover your company values, purpose, and mission. Review significant milestones in your history as well as the legends in your company. It is critical

to creating a sense of belonging. There isn't a marine alive who doesn't know who GySgt John Basilone was and he was killed over 70 years ago in 1945 during the battle for Iwo Jima.

7. Create or obtain soft skills training. There is no need to reinvent the wheel here. While at Priority Moving, I created my own customer service training, but I purchased a leadership program. If you can't find something that suits your needs, create it. Otherwise, it is better to purchase a reputable training package.

8. Train all of your existing team members. As you roll out your new training modules, make sure all of your existing personnel go through the same training. If you don't, they will undermine the training of your new hires because your veterans won't be following the procedures exactly. I guarantee it. They will tell the new hires something like, "I don't care how you were trained, here's how we do it."

9. Train the trainers. Training is a skill just like any other. When you invest in training your trainers, they are more comfortable presenting the material.

10. Video your training. By doing so, trainers can review and see how they did and make adjustments as necessary. There are days when you can't seem to find the right words and others when you will have the gift of gab. If you video your trainings you can then rehearse those golden phrases so they are delivered every time. Also, if your trainer can't deliver the training in person, the video allows for a non-trainer to proctor the training session using the video as the delivery tool.

Creating training takes time, but it is time well spent. Once completed, expect your team to respond and your company to prosper.

5. Defined Career Path

Alright, you are trying to grow your company, you've created clear job descriptions, you train your personnel, and you have provided clear, simple metrics, but, you haven't defined how people can grow within your organization? The result will be high turnover. Why?

Growth is a natural desire and state for most of us. The lack of a defined career path creates uncertainty in the minds of your team and doesn't provide safety. Maslow postulates that we want "...a predictable, orderly world."[17] Part of that predictability is the ability to control our own growth and destiny.

WII-FM, (**W**hat's **I**n **I**t **F**or **M**e) is everyone's favorite radio station. Salespeople know that if you don't tell prospective buyers how your goods or services can benefit them, then you will never make the sale. Ultimately, leadership is about selling your dream or vision to your team. It's about winning over the "Hearts and Minds" of your teammates. The more successful you are at this, the more "buy-in" your team has, the more inspired they become to help you fulfill this vision. When we speak of values and purpose, we are referring to the emotional benefits of the dream. Values and purpose will gain you their hearts, but career path delivers their minds.

As with corporate growth, we are either growing or dying, there is no status quo. Psychologically we know this at a deep and instinctive level. We are, at our core, pack animals. Our very survival as a species is centered around our ability to cooperate with each other. As pack animals, we have two desires. First, to know where we stand in the pack relative to the other pack members. Second, we have a need to be as high up the pack hierarchy as possible. The higher up the pack hierarchy we are, the more useful we are to the pack, the less expendable we are. Therefore, the ability to advance our career represents safety.

In a study between the relationship of career development and staff motivation published in the *Arabian Journal of Business and Management Review* in 2015, researchers Navern Pillay, Quraisha Dawood and Anis Karodia concluded that "...career advancement had a highly positive effect on motivation."[18] Although in their study, Pillay et al saw that "...the majority [of] respondents rated as high the motivation of employees after training. For these respondents took pride in the way they did their jobs, training boosted employees' confidence and satisfaction" there was also "...a significant number of respondents were not highly motivated after training."[19] For these, training alone was not sufficient but rather a means to an end, that of advancement.

When I took over at Priority Moving, I found a similar situation. When I arrived there, we had a nascent training program in place. Besides all new movers going through Basic Mover's Training, I quickly included courses in Customer Service and Packing, both necessary skills to be a well-rounded mover. As Pillay's study predicted, many of our movers took pride in acquiring additional skills and earning more money.

We were a growing company with an increasing fleet of trucks. Since we were a 7-day-a-week operation, each additional truck required 1-1/2 new crews. Lead movers were in short supply and most helpers didn't want the added responsibility of becoming a Lead. So, we added a class on leadership to the mix. We still struggled to get more Leads. It wasn't until we announced a new policy that only Lead movers would qualify for promotion to other roles like Training Manager, Quality Assurance, Wearhouse Supervisor, or Move Coordinator that we saw an increased interest in becoming a Lead Mover.

It turns out that most of our Movers saw moving as a job and not a career. It was a way to earn money, but not something many wanted to do for life. When we defined a career path, their perception changed. They now saw that if they qualified as a Lead, they could eventually move on to other things. They could attend a commercial driving class so they could get their class A license and drive a big rig. They could learn sales or move into operations. Since we were acquiring other moving companies, there were opportunities for new General Managers that knew our way of doing things. All of a sudden, they had careers and the opportunity to grow personally and take care of their families better.

The benefit to the company was equally as dramatic. We had a cadre of well-trained employees. The quality of our service, already high, improved even more. As managers, it was easier for us to distinguish our hard chargers as they sought out additional responsibility. When they were promoted, they reinforced our way of doing things.

My experience with Priority Moving is not unique. Christa Foley of Zappos Insights informed me that as of the writing of this book, they are revising the curriculum at Zappos University to include career path training. They've identified the skills needed for various career tracts and are creating a syllabus so that once a team member identifies where they want to work, they can gain exposure to the skills necessary to achieve it.

Our objective is to create an environment that meets our team members' need for safety and security. When we provide clear job descriptions, we tell them what they need to do. Good, simple metrics measure outcomes that team members can understand and control. An environment of corporate growth tells your team that there is opportunity for advancement in their career within your organization and they don't need to look elsewhere to find it. Finally, a defined career path gives them a map for advancement. As long as these opportunities are equally available to everyone, they will create an environment that satisfies your team's need for safety and security. This allows them to be open to feeling love and belonging, the next step in Maslow's Hierarchy.

CAREER PATH EXERCISE

Career paths don't need to be rigid, but they need some parameters. In general, the lower down the organizational chart someone enters the company, the more help they will need gaining the skills and experience to move up the ladder of success. To assist with this process:

1. Determine the skills needed to be a front-line supervisor (FLS)
2. Identify the skills required to be effective in each FLS position
3. Review subordinate rolls to each FLS and determine which positions provide an opportunity to develop the skills for each FLS
4. Develop or obtain additional training for each skill required by the FLS positions
5. Repeat this process for each subsequent managerial roll above the FLS

You now have some defined career paths. If someone joins your organization as a stock clerk and they want to become a floor manager, they can now see what training is required to advance in your organization. During your periodic one-to-one meetings, review their personal goals and help them achieve them by either facilitating a transfer to another position, provide training, or delegate a responsibility as discussed in Chapter 10.

PART IV

Execution

*"When one treats people with benevolence, justice, and righteous-
ness, and reposes confidence in them, the army will be united in
mind and all will be happy to serve their leaders."*

~ Sun Tzu, The Art of War

The morning of August 2, 1990 started off just like every
other morning of the previous six weeks. Life onboard the
U.S.S. Independence (CV-62) at sea is nothing but predictable. We had a saying, "Every day's a Monday." We were living
the movie *Groundhog Day*, but that was all about to change. In the
wardroom I picked up the ship's newspaper while I ate my break-
fast. The headline screams that the sovereign nation of Kuwait
had been invaded by Iraq. I remember turning to my shipmates
and saying, "Boys, we're going to war!" We spent the next 91
days planning and preparing for Operation Desert Storm. On

November 1, 1990 we were relieved by the U.S.S. Midway (CV-41) and started making our way back. Back home, my civilian friends didn't understand why I was so disappointed I didn't get to participate in the war.

There is nothing less satisfying than a job part done. You never see the payoff. For us, on the Indy, the payoff would have been helping kick Iraq out of Kuwait. Likewise, if you stop here, you'll never realize the value or the benefit of the work you've done so far. Many companies stop at this point. They create good job descriptions, they have the metrics, the training, the career path, and they are growing but they never experience the fullness of their work. They experience high turnover and chalk it up to outside influences. They work long hours and micromanage their team because they don't know any better. In Part IV, we'll discuss the Execution of Leadership. You'll discover how to leverage the preparation you did in Part III, maximize your influence, and inspire your team to greatness. You'll learn how to enrich people's lives and your own at the same time. Execution is where the magic happens.

In Part IV, we'll uncover how to create esprit de corps, that sense you belong to something special. I'll reveal the secret to creating a high-performing team and how to make sure everyone does their part willingly and eagerly.

CHAPTER 8

Third Tier Love and Belonging

*"From this day to the ending of the world, but we in it shall be
remembered. We few, we happy few, we band of brothers; For he
today that sheds his blood with me shall be my brother; be he ne'er
so vile, this day shall gentle his condition; and gentlemen
in England now-a-bed shall think themselves accursed they
were not here, and hold their manhoods cheap whiles any
speaks that fought with us upon Saint Crispin's day."*

~ William Shakespeare, Henry V

During three weeks in the summer of 1954 two separate buses
containing a dozen 12-year-old boys each, all strangers to
each other, pulled up to a Boy Scouts of America camp located
near Robbers Cave State Park in Oklahoma.[20] These groups were
the unknowing test subjects for a, now famous, experiment to test
how strangers might produce a group structure and how groups

compete for resources.[21] In the first phase of the experiment, the two groups were kept segregated and ignorant of each other's existence. When presented with common goals, each group of boys formed their own group structure, hierarchy, and culture. This occurred in less than a week.

These exact same conditions exist in every company. For the most part, although not always, employees are strangers to each other before they are hired. Left to their own devices, employees will find common goals and form their own group structure. It is human nature and the Robber's Cave Experiment confirmed it. Left on our own, people may find their own goals and they may differ from yours. Your sales department may just want to sell things regardless of whether or not the sale is good for the customer. Operations may decide their goal is to keep costs down, even if the customer suffers. Equally as bad, they may decide their goal is long hours since that usually means overtime pay and more money for them. This makes it easier for them to meet their physiological needs of feeding their family. People need guidance and you need a cohesive team so this doesn't happen.

Creating a Cohesive Team

While at a conference for professional speakers, I attended a breakout session of speakers with a military background. We were introducing ourselves, sharing our speech topics, and giving a synopsis of how our military experience shaped where we are today. There were veterans from every conflict since the Vietnam War and the sense of camaraderie was palpable. An Iraq and Afghanistan veteran would talk about a significant experience and a Vietnam Vet would chime in with complete understanding.

Whenever two veterans meet, the connection is almost tangible. Irrespective of the branch of service, rank, or when they served, there is an instant connection. You might think this is because veterans are such a select group, but that isn't it. In 2018 there are approximately 23M veterans and active duty personnel which represents around 7% of the U.S. population. By contrast, according to the National Center for Education Statistics, there are around 3.6M elementary and secondary school teachers. But the bond between educators, although present, is not as strong as the bond between veterans.

You might think it's the shared experience, to a degree that is true. But teachers also have shared experiences. Is it that veterans serve something larger than themselves? They are prepared to sacrifice self for country and they serve a higher purpose? Again, that is part, but not all of it. Teachers serve a higher purpose. Few go into teaching for recognition and glory. Most, if not all, of the teachers I know are in it for the children. They want to see the next generation succeed and be prepared for life. Many give personal time and money to see that their charges get the best education they can. Although most teachers' lives are not at risk like our military members are, they are still serving a greater good.

Of course, military pride is not reserved for Veterans, active duty members of the military have esprit de corps. According to the Merriam-Webster dictionary, esprit de corps refers to the common spirit existing in the members of a group and inspiring enthusiasm, devotion, and strong regard for the honor of the group. The term is French and literally means "Spirit of the Body."

The reason why veterans from all eras have a bond is because of a commitment made to each other to leave no one behind. This simple, but powerful message starts in training. Whether at boot camp, basic training, officer candidate school, or service academy, the message is the same:

- If one dies, we all die
- Leave no one behind
- Do you want to share a foxhole with them?
- Keep the faith

These are just some of the things you hear while going through some of the most stressful training imaginable. Although rare, death in training is not unheard of. We all are aware that risk doesn't end when basic training concludes. It actually becomes more possible, even during "peace" time.

The result, for all military members, is the same. At the core of our souls, everyone who wears the uniform knows that every other member is as committed as we are because we persevered when others did not. This creates a sense of community, of belonging.

Different service branches have capitalized on the elitism of serving. "The Few, The Proud, The Marines" and "Be All You Can Be" are just two of the more memorable and powerful service slogans from my lifetime. Serving together doesn't mean we all necessarily like each other. I've served with people I didn't like. But, we all did respect each other.

I was once sent to Fort Bliss in El Paso, TX for a joint planning meeting. Representatives from all four branches of the service were present. I was outside talking with a Navy Lt. Commander when an Army Staff Sergeant from the 82nd Airborne approached on the sidewalk. As he passed us, he executed a sharp and snappy salute while bellowing "Hooah." The salute is a military custom rendered from a subordinate to any commissioned officer. It is part of the military culture in every country and has existed in one form or another since the Roman legions. The "Hooah" is a U.S. Army tradition and part of their culture. His salute was a show of respect, his Hooah was a form of bragging, he was saying, "I'm Army and you're not!" He had pride in his unit and it showed.

There is, however, a deeper psychological reason for the bond service members experience. During training, the physical conditioning forces prospective members to endure a certain amount of pain. Physical Training, or "PT" as it is commonly referred to in the military, is also used as an accountability tool or punishment during training. If a Drill Instructor sees one member of their class marching out of step, the entire class may be required to do push-ups until exhaustion. I remember once having to do 300 hop-n-pops, similar to a burpee, because the person standing next to me had their uniform insignia on wrong (they did them too). Then there is survival training, where you may go days between meals. These evolutions, and many more like them, were painful to say the least. A 2014 study conducted at the University of New South Wales and University of Queensland shows how shared pain actually increases the bond between participants.[22]

The greater the pain—the greater the bond. That is why elite groups, with rigorous requirements to join and difficult-to-near-impossible training like the Army Rangers, Green Beret and Night Stalkers; Navy Seals; Marine Raiders, Marine Force Recon or Air Force Special Tactics tend to be closer and more bonded than less elite units. Each has their own unique subculture but is part of the larger branch and overall military culture. Culture defines the group and creates the sense of belonging.

In the military, the creation of esprit de corps starts on your first day of training. The experiences that service members go through, though not identical, are similar enough. I recall at Aviation Officer Candidate School saluting cars because they had a blue base pass. The pass in the window indicated they were owned by a commissioned officer. After receiving my commission, I heard enlisted personnel that went through Boot Camp talking about saluting torpedoes. While neither of these practices exist outside of training, they are repeated at every service academy, ROTC indoctrination, and enlisted basic training program in every service. They reinforce the importance of showing respect for a superior commissioned officer and the value of the chain of command. Top-performing civilian organizations emulate this.

According to Tony Hsieh, CEO of Zappos, "Customer Service is not a department, it's the company." To Zappos, this is not just a slogan; it is strongly reinforced. By requiring all employees to take the same training, regardless of position, it creates a common experience, like military training does for service members.

This is the essence of Maslow's Love and Belonging. We need to be part of something bigger than ourselves. This is an anthropological imperative for humans, a survival trait. As I mentioned earlier, at our core, we are pack animals. Although the toughest of us can survive alone, as a species, we have thrived as a group. Civilization is a direct result of our ability to function as part of a larger whole. Left to our own, we naturally form groups.

In the early 1980's, my wife was the first woman to work as a baggage handler for a major airline. She quickly became a union shop steward before getting a job at the union's national headquarters outside Washington, DC. She tells stories of employee strife that will have you shaking your head.

Her airline was divided into four separate groups, each with their own culture, values and agenda. The airline employees were represented by three different unions, the International Association of Machinists (IAM), the Brotherhood of Railway, Airline & Steamship Clerks (BRAC) and the Airlines Pilot Association. Then there were the executives and managers. These "groups" did not always work well together. The baggage handlers didn't work well with the gate agents, and the pilots were isolated. Even the executives and managers were at odds. The rumor was one of the airline's Presidents removed the bathroom stall doors in the executive restroom so the junior executives would get back to work quickly and not linger.

In part, these separate groups formed because of a lack of an intentional plan to create a cohesive team.

Developing Esprit De Corps

If you have never been part of an elite group, then you are truly missing out. It doesn't have to be a Special Operations Team. I'm referring to any winning sports team, debate team, or other team that has been recognized for outstanding success. I have had the good fortune of being a part of several of these. My high school swim team was undefeated for its 17th year in a row when I joined. VF-211, my last fleet squadron, had a storied past going back to WWII and had a rich history of receiving awards and accolades. Each of the elite teams I had the honor of being part of had one characteristic in common, an outward focus, a focus on others, not ourselves.

When I joined our swim team, I was constantly reminded of our alumni and our tradition of winning. It was never "don't let yourself down," but rather "don't let them down." In the Navy, it was about the mission, fleet, and other military elements we were supporting. Esprit de corps, like happiness, doesn't come from focusing inward but rather on focusing outwards. Companies need to know what higher purpose they are serving.

Each company and organization that survives and has a customer base serves a higher purpose. It doesn't matter if there is stiff competition in the marketplace. Despite the competition, you still serve a higher purpose. Organizations of any kind only exist because they add value. That value is a clue to what your higher purpose may be. Let's explore this concept.

Money is nothing more than an IOU for work performed. In the early days of civilization, we bartered or traded goods and services. If you were good at raising sheep, and I was good at building structures, you might trade me some of your sheep if I built you a pen. What if I needed sheep, but you didn't need any structures built, however, you needed a hinge forged for your sheep pen gate? I don't know how to forge steel, but the smithy does and he needs a new shed to store his raw iron ore. So, I build the shed, he forges you a hinge, and you give me a sheep—easy. This worked well when communities were small. As communities grew larger, it became more difficult to manage the barter system. As a result, people traded valuable goods for work, gems, precious metals, etc. Eventually, this became money. Therefore, money is nothing more than an IOU for work you performed. It is redeemable anywhere for whatever goods or services you need.

For example, let's take iron ore. In its raw form, it isn't good for much, it's a rock. You can throw it as a projectile to kill an animal or ward off an attack, but it isn't good for much else. Not knowing what to do with it, you wouldn't trade much of your hard work for it. However, if you know how to forge it into iron rods or ingots, a smith can now make iron tools. Since tools allow us to be more efficient, they have value to us (assuming we know how to use the tool). If you know how to turn iron into steel, the value increases even more. Steel, being less brittle than iron, makes better tools. However, your higher purpose isn't just making tools. Your higher purpose is the impact you have on your community. In our example, tools allow us to be more efficient, therefore, we can create a larger community since our work efforts, whether it is farming, hunting, or building, will enable us to support more people. From a historic perspective, larger communities are generally safer. A family living on an isolated farmstead was at risk from natural disasters as well as bandits or marauders from another region. If the family was part of a community, they could help each other in the case of a natural disaster or band together to defend against invaders. The larger the community, the more resources, the better equipped they were to respond, and the safer they were. Therefore, the higher purpose for a business that makes tools may be "making our community a safer place."

If you worked for this manufacturer, would you work harder if you knew, with certainty, that your efforts helped your neighbors, friends, and family live in a safer community? Of course, you would.

When I started at Priority Moving, we didn't know what our higher purpose was. We knew we moved people. As I mentioned earlier, we put in training programs and procedures designed to minimize mistakes, improve our customers' experience, and make us more efficient. Initially, compliance was spotty.

Recognizing the problem, the senior management team and I started working on "why" we were in business, what was our higher purpose. This was a somewhat free-form discussion. At that time, we didn't have a value statement or any defined core values. We had values, they just weren't articulated. Note that every entity has values, but sometimes they are only implied. We had a set of procedures designed to reflect our implicit values of honesty, service to customers, and respect for others.

We then asked ourselves a simple question, "Why are we doing these things?" We looked at why we did them for the customer and for our teammates. When we got to it, the answer was startlingly simple and clearly true for each of us in senior management. Our purpose was to reduce stress. Moving is one of the most stressful things we do in life. Besides the stress of packing all our possessions by a certain deadline, we change our living environment and routine. There's the added stress of having strangers in your home handling your possessions, the uncertainty if the movers will show up, and the risk of damage to treasures and heirlooms. The list goes on.

At Priority Moving, we trained our movers on every aspect of our business. They learned how to protect furniture, pack boxes properly, proper lifting techniques, proper carrying techniques, communicating while carrying heavy goods, protecting the property, loading the truck, filling out the paperwork, collecting payment, what to do in the event of non-payment, how to answer the phone, how to schedule a move, how to create invoices, how to handle payroll, and more. The training served to reduce the stress on our employees by ensuring they knew exactly how to do their jobs.

Our policies were likewise designed to reduce stress. For example, time-off requests of up to one week from movers were approved as long as they had a reasonable plan to have their work covered and there was no overriding reason to say no.

Without argument, we gave refunds to unhappy customers if they requested it. At first, this was a controversial policy because the customer's perception wasn't always accurate. We realized if we argued back, we almost always gave them some refund and they walked away unsatisfied. So, we started asking our customers what we could do to make them happy. This took courage on our part. At first, we thought we would be giving away a lot of moves. The reality is, by training our team to provide great customer service, we rarely had a problem. When we did, the customer rarely wanted a full refund. By acquiescing quickly and without argument, we reduced the customers' and our own stress while keeping more customers.

We had a Quality Board that met anytime there was a significant service failure where a customer requested monetary compensation. The Board consisted of the Operations Manager, Warehouse Manager (both of whom were experienced movers), and me. We brought the crew that performed the move into the conference room. Without disclosing the customer complaint, we requested they review the entire move from start to finish. We would ask about every procedure and then analyze whether or not we had a policy issue.

In the case of a policy issue, we would amend our policy as appropriate and then promulgate the change and train on it. Regarding personnel issues, we decide if additional training would help. If a crewman had a history of service problems, we determined if the mover needed to be held accountable in another way, up to and including termination.

By holding this Quality Board, our policies and procedures got so tight that service failures became few and far between. Weak teammates either became stronger or left the company. As our quality improved, both our crew and our customers suffered less stress.

When we analyzed everything we did, we realized that we had nailed our purpose. We were a company that reduced stress, during one of life's most stressful events, moving. The final test centered around Bryan, the owner and CEO of the company. He is a great guy who built a great company, but when I came on board, it had stagnated. One of the problems was that Brian was easily distracted. Brian wants to take care of people—he's a good person. When employees had a problem, he would drop what he was doing and try to help by making their life a little less stressful. When one of his three teenage kids would call with a problem, he reacted the same way, even if it could have waited until after work. Bryan is all about helping people. This was critical. Our purpose had to align with Bryan's values or he would have undercut everything we attempted. Since our purpose aligned with his, we knew we nailed it.

Once we knew our purpose, we kept this in mind with everything we did. When hiring, we attracted people who related to the purpose. During training, we highlighted how the processes and procedures were stress reducers. We vetted our vendors by their ability to facilitate this purpose. We shared our purpose in our marketing and sales efforts. This attracted customers that wanted as little stress during their move as possible and were willing to pay for it.

As we solidified our purpose, so did our team. When we hired experienced movers from other companies, they would frequently want to do things their way. When correcting them, I would hear our veteran team members say, "That's not the Priority Way!" We created an elite team and everyone, even our competitors, knew it. Our movers frequently received huge tips from our customers because of our excellent service. As a result, they were extremely loyal to us although we paid slightly less than our competitors. If movers left to work elsewhere for more money, often they'd return, or attempt to return, upon realizing they weren't being held to the same standards and, therefore, not receiving the same tips.

Finally, every time a new procedure or policy was proposed, it was tested against our purpose. If the proposed change might increase stress, it was rejected. If it didn't affect stress, we looked for ways to change the policy to reduce stress. We only implemented the new procedure or policy if it helped reduce stress.

It is evident that our purpose was the cause of this success. The company was sold at the close of 2013, to someone with decades of experience in the moving business. According to him, he purchased Priority Moving because of our dominance in the local moving market. He immediately changed our policies, procedures, and did away with all the training. He stopped talking about reducing stress and began focusing on increasing profits. The results? With the same staff, at least at first, he experienced significant service failures costing him more money, thereby reducing profits. After making further changes, additional stress caused personnel turnover and further degrading profits. Although they are still in business, they lost their dominance in the market and are now just another moving company.

Understanding our higher purpose and then vetting our people, policies, and procedures against it gave everyone a sense of pride in what they were doing. Pride is esprit de corps. As our esprit grew, we attracted good people who valued what we did and wanted to be a part of it. These people were customers who were willing to pay more, vendors who were willing to help more, and team members who were willing to do more. We created a community and fulfilled everyone's need for Love and Belonging.

Take the time to figure out your higher purpose. Once you do, vet all of your policies and procedures against it. Ask, "Do they help, hinder or have no effect on your ability to achieve this purpose?" If they hinder, get rid of them. If they have no effect, modify them. Each policy and procedure needs to advance your higher purpose. When you incorporate your purpose into your hiring process, it makes sure your team supports this purpose. Use it as a litmus test for any disciplinary action. Make sure your vendors all support your higher purpose or at worst, don't hinder your purpose. Your purpose is a framework for your marketing message. Talk about it in every company communication. Make sure your team is proud to deliver this purpose and create the esprit de corps your team needs.

Purpose-Built Culture

A purpose-built culture is one of the best ways to create a sense of love and belonging. Culture is a celebration of our values. In society, there are seven elements to culture:

- social organization – this is our family structure and social classes;
- language – this is more than just what language we speak but goes to the idioms we use and regional jargon;
- religion – representing how we justify our existence and the meaning of life;
- art and literature – how we entertain ourselves;
- form of government – our method for creating and enforcing our laws;
- economic system – our method of producing and distributing goods and services; and
- customs and traditions – the way we celebrate aspects of our lives together.

For the most part, these same elements exist in a company or organization's culture.

Social Organization

Social structure can refer to how we segregate the personnel within the organization. Onboard a U.S. Navy ship, there is:

- Admiral's Country or Flag Country where the Admiral and staff live and work,

- Officer's Country where commissioned officers live and eat, and
- Chief's Country where the Chief Petty Officers live and eat.

Enlisted personnel don't enter any of these areas unless they have official business there. They don't take shortcuts through them to get to other spaces either. Similarly, commissioned officers and Chief Petty Officers respect each other's and the Admiral's domain by not entering them without reason. I witnessed similar cultural divides in civilian life. In Tijuana, Mexico I visited a maquiladora plant where they had an executive dining room with an excellent Executive Chef. They had a separate employee dining room for everyone else. On the other extreme, there's Zappos, where there are no managers and all roles are equal. Years ago, I made a sales call on a credit rehabilitation company. Back in the late 1990's the norm in San Diego was referring to each other on a first name basis, irrespective of title. In contrast, at this company all the managers were referred to as Mr. or Ms. and their last name. That was part of their culture.

Your social organization needs to reflect your values. If your company values structure, your social organization may be one where no one jumps the chain of command without great cause. For example, if you have a good idea, you present it to your boss who then decides if they should implement the idea. They then pass it on up the chain of command for a decision or sit on it and quash the idea all together. The military is very much like this.

A less structured value system, like Zappos, has a completely different social structure. Zappos values flexibility. Tony Hsieh, the CEO of Zappos, feared the inflexibility of bureaucracy that usually comes with larger organizations. As a result, he adopted Holacracy, the purported next evolution in management where managers don't exist. Instead, team members take on roles that are fluid and dynamic. Roles may be permanent or temporary. Your abilities determine whether or not you get a role and not your title. It is an extremely flat social structure.

Language

Most companies and organizations have their own language. They have their own idioms, jargon, and slang. In the military, it is common to hear "roger that" as an acknowledgement. This derives from radio etiquette where the response of "roger" means that you heard the previous transmission. Another common military phrase is "Whiskey Tango Foxtrot" which refers to the international alpha-phonetic alphabet. This method uses specific words that start with the first letter you want to spell in order to avoid confusion. Whisky is "W," Tango is "T," and Foxtrot is "F" so "Whiskey Tango Foxtrot" is "WTF" or "what the f____," which indicates dismay or sometimes shock. It isn't unusual for companies or industries to develop their own slang.

Once again, language reflects the actual values of the organization. When I was in the moving industry, we moved possessions, never stuff or junk. Movers recognize the value in the word "possessions." Imagine that you overhear your mover saying to another mover, "I'll get the junk in the bedroom." You probably would worry about them respecting your possessions the way you would like. In fact, language becomes such an ingrained part of a company's culture. Salespeople are repeatedly warned about not using jargon when they are speaking with prospects and customers.

LOCKED ON LANGUAGE EXERCISE

1. Make a list of your industry jargon.
2. Make a list of the terms you find yourself explaining to customers or new vendors who are not in your industry.

3. Create a focus group of industry outsiders, give them the list of words, out of context, and ask them to explain what they mean, and how they feel about them.
4. Use the words in a common sentence and ask them the same questions.
5. Identify the words that are either a) misunderstood or b) generally connote a feeling that is contrary to your values.
6. Develop new terms for the listener that reflect your company's values (e.g., say possessions, not junk or stuff).
7. Train your staff to use only these terms. Put them in your training manuals and immediately correct anyone who uses the wrong term.
8. Empower others to correct everyone in the company, regardless of position. At Priority Moving, if someone said stuff or junk, whoever heard them corrected them. As a new Vice President, I was corrected by movers who had less education, made considerably less money, and had no authority whatsoever, all to my betterment.

If you are going to have a purpose-built culture, you need purpose-built language. Create it, teach it, enforce it, and use it.

Religion

In societal culture, religion is how we give meaning to life. In business, this is our higher purpose. When we define our organization's higher purpose, we strengthen our culture. This becomes a gauge to measure every aspect of our organization. If you have ever met someone that is evangelical about their religion, you know that it permeates every aspect of their life. All of their thoughts, words, and deeds are measured, weighed, and judged against their religious precepts.

If you have identified your organization's higher purpose, it serves the same role as religion. If utilized properly, it becomes

enmeshed in your culture. During meetings, use your higher purpose as a gauge to see if your policies and procedures are being
followed. Benchmark your decisions on your higher purpose and
your team will do the same.

While at Priority Moving, I asked a Lead Mover why he opted
to transport nine potted trees in the truck. We always advised
against this since:

1) live plants don't thrive in the back of a hot 26' box truck,
   and
2) pots are not made to be shipped full of dirt as they tend to
   break.

In this instance, the pots did break and we were talking about
why the mover chose to move them. His response, "The shipper
was stressing out how to get her trees to her new home." Since
the mover was in a potential no-win situation he did not get in
trouble. It wasn't strictly against policy to move plants, just ill-
advised. As a result, we changed our policy and procedure so our
movers weren't put in this situation again. The fact that the mover
knew his job was to reduce stress meant our messaging about our
purpose had permeated the organization. As a result, people were
making decisions with that in mind.

Now it's time to weave your higher purpose into the fabric of
your organization and build your culture around it.

Art & Literature

The art & literature of society speaks to your physical environment.
It is an expression of a culture's mores, values, thoughts, and beliefs.
From early petroglyphs, through the Russian icons to Jackson Pol-
lack and Andy Warhol, art reflects the culture of the time.

The décor and layout of your organization achieves the
same. Naval vessels are starkly utilitarian and reflect the fact that

accomplishing missions is more important than creature comforts. They are stark in appearance, stink like machine oil, and hum with the sound of machinery. There is no doubt that serious business is conducted onboard a ship of war. A squadron's ready room is decorated with mementos of the unit's accomplishments, photographs of aircraft in various flight regimes, and a general celebration of honor and bravery. War is hard, and there is nothing soft onboard a warship.

Similar environmental illustrations of values can be found in civilian companies. I visited a maquiladora heavily vested in Kaizen, the Japanese philosophy of efficiency, developed and made popular by Toyota. Each of their desks were set up exactly the same. If you were at someone's desk and needed a writing implement, you knew you would find in the top right-hand side drawer exactly one black pen, one blue pen, one red pen, and one pencil. No one had the ubiquitous collection of mismatched logo pens provided by suppliers. All desks were arranged in the exact same manner with <u>no</u> personal items displayed. In their maintenance shop, the tool rack had an outline of where each tool was to be placed. Toolboxes contained foam cutouts. At a glance, you knew if a tool was in use or not. This extended to their manufacturing floor where outlines on the floor indicated where items were to be stored and people were to walk. Kaizen was a deep and ingrained part of their culture, and the layout and design of their facility reflected this fact.

Creative organizations, like software companies, marketing companies, and video production companies are frequently located in buildings with open space designs that facilitate the free flow of ideas. Inspiring art or architectural elements abound.

A client in Fort Collins, Colorado complained about not being able to hire good plumbers that were well organized and meticulous. His office was a mess, with stuff piled on every flat surface and his warehouse was nothing more than shelves filled with junk with no rhyme or reason. He probably interviewed countless organized and meticulous plumbers, but none of them would have been attracted to or willing to work at his office.

When I was hired by Priority Moving, the office was similar to the plumbers. Slowly, as we put the new procedures in place that made us more organized, our environment changed as well. We organized and rearranged. We digitized all of the paperwork and stored it in a new, well-organized computer network. Before we reorganized, it wasn't uncommon for us to spend hours looking for misplaced paperwork. When completed, our lobby had a facelift. It presented us as the well-organized and highly efficient company we had become. Everything in our new environment reinforced our values and stressed organization, one of the keys to conducting an efficient and successful move.

Make sure your environment reflects your values. If you are a severe company, your décor should not be frivolous. If you are creative, be whimsical. If organization is critical, be organized. When one element of your culture is out of sync with the rest, it creates discord and damages your integrity, even if only subliminally. Why risk diminishing your integrity at all?

Form of Government

How are decisions made in your company? Is it top-down or bottom-up? When I was the President of the moving company, we clearly had a bottom-up culture. Everyone was empowered to make decisions that were consistent with our values and purpose. If management wanted to make a change, we presented the team with the problem and let them develop a solution. When we sold the company, the new owners changed to a top-down culture. Shortly after the acquisition, in my new role of General Manager, I was discussing a software scheduling problem with our Executive VP. I mentioned that I would bring it up at our next weekly staff meeting. She responded that we needed a solution first. I thought the staff was better suited to develop a solution as they were the ones doing the work. I was overruled.

This was a complete departure from our former culture. Within six months, 50% of the office workers left the company. By the end of the year, that number was closer to 90%. The people that left thrived in the bottom-up culture where our higher purpose was to reduce stress for all. The new owners believed that our purpose was to move people's possessions, not remove stress. Because of the shortage of movers, they believed the more movers the better, even if they weren't particularly good movers. The top-down culture added stress to our team, causing the high turnover. The focus on movers over customers meant our repeat business dropped off considerably. All of this happened because our form of governance changed and our culture changed.

Economic System

Your economic system helps shape your culture. In a capitalistic society, we reward based on merit as determined by the populace as a whole. If enough people see the value of your service at the price requested, they reward you by purchasing your goods or services. Contrast this with the Communist/Socialist system where the culture is regardless of effort, you get what you need. In this system, the result is few people feel compelled to give everything or try hard. This philosophy applies to companies, too.

For businesses and organizations, your economic system is your method of compensation which includes any raises and bonuses. For many of my coaching clients, this starts as a time-based compensation system. That is, the longer someone is at the company, the more money they make. This puts ownership under enormous strain. One of the first questions new clients ask me is how can they afford to give their guys a raise when it's time for reviews. The problem with a time-based compensation system is that it rewards longevity over productivity. It creates a culture where not making waves is rewarded more than being innovative and taking chances. Bonuses are usually random and capricious.

A merit-based economic system supports growth and innovation. In merit-based systems, employees receive an increase in compensation when they demonstrate they provide more value by gaining new skills or increasing their worth in other ways. Each position within your organization exists for a reason which does <u>not</u> include providing someone with a job. Employees are like any other business expense; they serve to either generate or increase revenue or reduce or minimize expenses or liabilities. As such, you require a return on investment for hiring them. This is why having clear job descriptions and simple metrics is so important. The Locked On Key Accountabilities Exercise in Chapter 7 tells you why each position exists. Metrics provide the means to understand the return you can expect for each position. Once you know the return, then you can value their effort. Regardless of how good someone gets at a job, their worth in that position is only so much. Part of this calculation is how easy they are to replace. That is why low-skilled labor, such as a general laborer at a construction site, is cheaper than high-skilled labor like an electrician or finish carpenter.

I recommend creating a schedule of compensation for each position with a minimum and maximum possible pay. In most cases, you can tie the raises with increased skills until someone reaches the maximum pay. We set up such a schedule for our movers. Movers started at minimum wage. They immediately went through BMT (Basic Mover Training). As they progressed through other trainings, they received incremental raises. Only after going through all the training, were they eligible for promotion to Lead Mover. This way, if they wanted to earn more money, they had to provide more value. Raises based on longevity are advisable when you are at risk of not having enough staff because your competitors are paying significantly more. However, this doesn't mean you have to pay at the going rate, per se. As noted, we paid our movers slightly less than our competitors, but they stayed or returned because of our superior working conditions. Keep in mind that in all the various polls and studies I've read, pay is never one of the top five reasons for leaving a job.

Customs and Traditions

Customs and traditions can come about organically or be purposefully built. In navies around the world, whenever a ship crosses the equator there is a "Crossing the Line" ceremony. Sailors that have not previously been south of the equator are inducted into the "Order of Neptune" and transform from a "slimy Pollywog" to a "trusty Shellback."

Pinning on your wings and drinking your wings are two organic traditions of the U.S. Navy. When you earn your wings, in a ceremony you are presented with your wings and they are placed on your uniform, usually by someone close to you. In my case, my parents jointly pinned on my wings. The ceremony is an example of a purpose-built tradition. However, after putting the wings on my uniform, my father slapped them onto my chest, causing the pins to puncture the cheap backing clasps and pierce my skin. This tradition has evolved organically.

Another organic tradition around earning your wings is "drinking your wings." Your new wings are dropped into a mug of beer and then you catch the wings in your teeth as you drink the beer. As we celebrated into the evening, after formally receiving my wings, I alternated between having to drink my wings and having them pinned back on again after drinking them. Although I have no idea who started these traditions, no doubt they were not designed by the U.S. Navy. In any case, I awoke the next morning with a hangover and two pin pricks on my sore left chest.

Civilian companies have traditions as well, although fewer of them. About 15 months after leaving the Navy, I got my first civilian job as an "adult" selling telecommunications equipment.

Shortly after I started at the company, the owner came in and rang a bell on the receptionist desk. I was told it meant that he closed a deal. I was the only other salesperson besides him and had yet to make a sale. I longed for the day when I would ring that bell. Weeks went by and still no sale. Meanwhile, the owner would periodically come in and ring the bell. I worked hard and kept getting in front of many potential customers, but my first sale was elusive. Although I was warmly greeted by the team every morning, I didn't feel truly part of the team. Four months after starting, I closed my first deal. It wasn't very large, but it was a sale. I burst in the front door and rang that bell enthusiastically and received the congratulations of the entire team. The very next day, I did it again. Ringing the bell was one of our traditions. Even though only salespeople rang the bell, everyone else participated in the celebration that followed. The owner started the bell tradition because he wanted everyone to know the importance of sales and felt they were worthy of a celebration. After all, everyone's jobs, not just the salesperson's job, depended on continued sales.

About 2-1/2 years later, I moved to our biggest rival. When I got there, they didn't have a tradition like ringing the bell. Being a seasoned salesperson at this point, it didn't take me long to close my first deal. When I got back to the office, the Controller, Myra, asked me for the deposit check from the customer. On a whim, I held it up like you would a bone for a dog when you are trying to teach them to sit and I said, "Bark like a dog." Myra, being a fun-loving, all-around good person held her front hands up like a dog begging and proceeded to bark to everyone's laughter. A tradition was born. After that, every time I closed a deal, I would hold the check up for Myra and she would bark and act like a dog begging before I turned it in. Soon, all the salespeople were doing it.

Although you probably don't want to dictate every aspect of your culture, you definitely want to shape and guide it. Create one or two fun traditions that highlight what is important to your organization. The traditions must support your core values and not undercut them. When I went through my Crossing the Line, one of the traditions was for the Shellback on the ship to make shillelaghs. They would do this by cutting a firehouse into 18" lengths and wrapping duct tape around one end so they can hold it like a baton. They would also dress up as pirates. When the ceremony began, all of us pollywogs were told to wear our uniforms inside out with our underwear on the outside. Then we were forced to crawl on our hands and knees around the ship to various purification stations so we could enter Neptune's kingdom and become a Shellback. While we were going through this evolution, we were "motivated" by the existing Shellbacks with their shillelaghs. This was a tradition that had been around for centuries. In days past, sailors had to be tougher than they are today and the ceremonies were more painful, physically demanding, and potentially dangerous. As hazing incidents around the country started getting negative national press, the Navy chose to tone down the ceremony to be in line with the current naval culture.

As a leader, you should create your own cultural traditions. They can be small and informal like the ringing of the bell or larger and more elaborate like Crossing the Line. A military tradition that dates back to the Roman Legions is the "Dining Out" or "Dining In" dinners. I was a Junior Officer the first time I was introduced to a Dining Out. The Skipper announced the specific date and provided us with the "rules of engagement." This massive book contained all the rules and etiquette for Dining Out. That's right, rules. A Dining Out is a highly structured, formal event requiring formal dress. There is a Master of Ceremonies, called Mr. or Madame Vice, typically a Junior Officer, responsible for enforcing proper protocol; the President of the Mess, a Senior Officer, usually the Commanding Officer who resides over the ceremony; a grog bowl filled with…grog; skits, usually by the Junior Officers at the expense of the Senior but sometimes vice-versa; and a lengthy list of rules including when you can drink, how to propose a toast, when you can leave the room to go to the head (bathroom) and how to ask permission, what happens if you break a rule, fines, etc. At first, it can be extremely intimidating and first-time attendees approach it with dread. However, once you have been to a Dining Out, you look forward to the next one. You can adapt the Dining Out in a way that upholds your culture.

The Dining Out celebrates discipline by exaggerating it to become farcical. Through the skits, it allows Junior Officers to vent some of their frustrations in a humorous and safe way without fear of retribution. Smart Commanding Officers use a Dining Out to develop bonds, create a greater sense of belonging through a shared experience, and enhance the feeling of love and belonging. They do this while simultaneously gathering feedback about the morale of their officers by the content of the skits.

Quarters

The Squadron Duty Officer or SDO, comes smartly to attention and bellows, "Squad-ron, atten-hut!". As one, the approximately 150 officers and sailors of Fighter Squadron two-eleven come sharply to attention. The SDO executes a sharp left face towards the approaching Commanding Officer, with his Command Master Chief in tow. "Sir, Fighter Squadron Two-One-One all present or accounted for." So begins "Quarters," a formal way to muster your troops, make sure everyone is accounted for, and "pass the word," which is Navy jargon for making sure everyone knows what is going on. In a fighter squadron, Quarters are common, but not necessarily conducted on a set schedule. Quarters celebrate accomplishments and also sends a powerful subliminal message, "We are one unit." When the skipper calls Quarters and tells the squadron that we are going to be working "port and starboard," two shifts working 12 hours on and 12 hours off, the skipper is saying, "I care about you and I want you to understand why we are asking this of you." After being at sea for a grueling 111 days (but who's counting) during Operation Desert Shield, the buildup for Operation Desert Storm, our skipper held Quarters to say, "We're going into Singapore for liberty call. I know you have pent up steam, but let's make sure we respect the Singaporeans. Remember, each of you are an ambassador of the United States." He was actually saying, "I care about you and I don't want you to get into trouble."

Although I don't think your company or organization needs to "snap to" when holding company meetings, consider having some sort of custom associated with your informal gatherings. It should be something unique to your culture that everyone can grab onto and say, "That's ours." Company meetings are one of the best ways to develop cohesion. It avoids the perception of favorites by letting some people know what is going on. It also avoids implementation problems when "the word" isn't spread evenly. Finally, it creates a sense of what Chris Fussell and C.W. Goodyear, authors of *One Mission – How Leaders Build a Team of Teams*, calls a "shared consciousness," which is "a state in which all members have a common understanding of their mutually held problem set, shared access to key information, and are aligned in the direction they need to move next."[23]

In my coaching practice, I urge my clients, regardless of business size, to hold regular meetings. Frequently, the response is either, "I don't have time" or "I can't wait for the information." Almost always the opposite is true. A well-structured meeting passes information efficiently and frequently eliminates misinformation that can cause some costly mistakes. If you believe you can't wait for the information, test that assertion. First, ask yourself what's the longest you will have to wait for the information? If you are meeting weekly, then it's seven days. Next, ask what information you need that can't wait for seven days or what harm comes from my waiting for seven days to act on the information.

Most of the time, the answer is, it doesn't change a thing. If you realize you need information more frequently, then consider more frequent meetings. They don't need to be long, but they do need to be structured.

Frequency of meetings is not dependent on organization size. When I was the VP of Operations at Communications Plus, we held a weekly company-wide meeting. About 20 souls would gather in the operations office once a week, discuss the upcoming jobs, talk about issues with customers, vacation schedules, if applicable, and let people know about any upcoming company events. Everyone knew what was going on and no one felt left out. Furthermore, an opportunity for cross-department help arose. Sometimes customer service reps had a question about a feature that the installation technicians could answer. It prevented wasted time and sometimes, embarrassment.

In larger organizations, companywide meetings may be more difficult, but with modern technology like video conferencing and broadband internet, it is possible. In General McChrystal's book, *Team of Teams: New Rules of Engagement for a Complex World*, he details how he held daily video briefings that spanned the entire 60,000-member Special Operations Command with participants literally around the world. It had an amazing, powerful and positive effect on our ability to successfully prosecute the War on Terror.

The bottom line, regular effective meetings and ad hoc ceremonies help unite people into a team and a community. Make them a part of your culture.

The best leaders create cohesive teams. Our inherent survival needs, as defined by Abraham Maslow, require this. To do this, you need to intentionally craft a unifying purpose. This purpose will create esprit de corps, a feeling amongst your team that they are special and serve something beyond themselves. Then you have to create a purpose-built culture that celebrates your values.

Make sure these values are reflected in your social structure, language, governance structure, physical environment, compensation policies, and finally your customs and traditions. When you do this, you will create a sense of love and belonging that is unified, cohesive, and pervasive within your organization. Having this structure allows your team to flourish and thrive in the fourth and final stage of Esteem.

CHAPTER 9

Fourth Tier Esteem

"...It is a proud privilege to be a soldier–a good soldier...[with]
discipline, self-respect, pride in his unit and his country, a high sense
of duty and obligation to comrades and to his superiors, and a self-
confidence born of demonstrated ability."

~ GEN. GEORGE S. PATTON, JR.

Your team should be coalescing nicely if at this point you have started hiring properly and are setting your team up for success with:

- clear and accurate job descriptions,
- solid metrics that they have control over,
- great training,
- a defined career path and a culture of corporate growth,
- a defined higher purpose and the creation of esprit de corps,

- effective meetings, and
- ad hoc celebrations of success.

If you have all of this in place, it is not time to rest on your laurels. The glue that holds this all together is your ability to create esteem in your team.

The word *esteem* comes from the Latin "aestimare" for to "value, determine the value of, appraise" and was originally used similarly like we use the word "estimate" today. I like to think of it as how we value or appraise other's contribution or worth to the group. When we hold someone in high esteem, we value them greatly. Likewise, someone we regard with low esteem is not of sufficient value.

When Maslow talks about our "Esteem Needs" he is referring to our group's recognition of our value to the group. From a survival perspective, we see that Maslow got it right. Our initial physiological needs of food, water, and regulation of our body temperature is further enhanced when our safety needs are met. We take dangerous risks to procure food and water when needed. However, if we can protect ourselves from the elements, and defend against sickness, injuries, or fellow humans who take our resources and make it more difficult to obtain food and water, then we are reinforcing our physiological needs by meeting our safety needs. Likewise, becoming a part of a group and feeling loved and a sense of belonging, affords us more safety and allows us to be more efficient in our food gathering. Therefore, we are better able to meet our physiological requirements. Being held in high esteem, or being seen as a valued contributor to the group, cements our membership in the group. This improves our chance of continued survival.

Even though we live in an abundance society, where most of our physiological and safety needs are met by society as a whole, we still have deep-seated needs to be part of a group. We want to be valued as a contributor to the group. To keep your team together and help your members become self-actualized, value the members of your team in a positive and constructive way. To maximize your team's sense of esteem, use one-on-one meetings, recognition, delegation, and accountability.

Locked On Tip

Creating esteem in an individual or a team won't work if you don't have everything else in place first. Let your team know you are committed to meeting their lower-level needs. In fact, you can't even properly recognize an achievement nor hold someone accountable for a failure unless you have first substantially met your team's safety needs and developed a sense of love and belonging.

One-to-One Meetings

The simplest and most effective way to show the esteem in which you hold a team member is to spend time with them. When they say time is money, nothing can be farther from the truth. While many people trade time for money, and therefore, equate the two, time is by far the more valuable resource. There is a simple way to test this. If a bad decision ends up costing you $1,000, you can always recover that money in the future by some other means. If, on the other hand, a bad decision ends up costing you one day, you will never get that day back. It doesn't matter who you are or how wealthy you are, it's gone. We all know this intuitively. This is why we value the time someone spends with us so highly.

I'm not talking about hanging out and socializing. It's not that these activities are necessarily bad, in fact, they also promote esteem. However, they can also foster resentment if you favor one team member over another. I often tell my clients that employees are like children and pets, they need clear boundaries set and they crave your positive attention. You can provide that attention in a constructive environment by holding a regular, one-to-one meeting with each of your team members.

Don't confuse a one-to-one meeting with a casual conversation. Casual conversations, while important, don't carry the same weight as they aren't planned. The power of the one-to-one meeting is that they are scheduled. When you, as a leader, block out specific time to meet with one of your team members you send a powerful subliminal message that the team member is important to you.

The Real Strategic Objective of the One-to-one

In my experience, the one-to-one meeting is the most misunderstood leadership tactic. A simple web search uncovers pages of advice on how to conduct an effective one-to-one revealing differing reasons to hold the meeting, but most miss the mark. They mistakenly highlight the positive byproducts of a well run one-to-one meeting as the reason for the meeting. In other words, they focus on the wrong objective. When you focus on the wrong objective, you get the wrong results.

The purpose of a one-to-one is to show your team members that they are important to you and you are invested in them and their success. As a result, you will benefit from a plethora of positive collateral outcomes. As your team becomes more comfortable knowing you are vested in their success, they will open up and help you help them. These meetings allow them to be candid about their aspirations, open about problems and challenges on the job, and become proactive in improving operations. In short, properly held one-to-ones reveal the barriers to your team's success, both personal and organizational. When you remove these barriers, you propel your people and your organization to stratospheric heights.

Conducting a One-to-one Meeting

Idle chitchat should start out each one-to-one meeting. Except it isn't really idle, it is, in fact, purposeful. This is your time to create or reinforce the bond between you and your team member.

Make sure you put your team member at ease. Don't hold the meeting from behind a desk as it creates a barrier between the two of you. If you have casual chairs or a sitting area, use that. Make it feel like someone's living room and not an office visit. Sit side by side with your chairs angled towards each other so you can make eye contact. Don't face them head-on as this makes it feel too confrontational. Have and offer refreshments, preferably something they enjoy. Many offices have outside eating areas or atriums. If you use a public area like these, make sure you can ensure privacy. As you will be asking personal questions, make sure the environment is one where your team members feel safe about telling you things without being overheard.

If this is one of your first meetings with a subordinate, take the time to learn who they are personally. Use active listening and ask them about themselves. You probably found out some personal things during the interview; this is the time to dig deeper or fill in the blanks. In subsequent meetings, ask about what's going on with their family in a friendly way, the way two friends might share.

As marital status or family status questions are off limits during the interview, you can now ask about the names of their children or spouse. You can also touch upon hobbies, past accomplishments, and activities of interest. Make it a casual conversation and let it flow naturally. Use open-ended questions and listen to the answers so you can ask good follow-up questions. Don't be in a hurry. Don't use a written agenda for these early meetings as it sends the wrong message.

In a first meeting, you may not learn as much as you want to about your new team member, but that's ok. It takes time to build trust and rapport. You'll learn more in each subsequent meeting. When the personal conversation slows down, transition to business. An easy way to do this is first ask about their aspirations. This is a natural bridge from personal to business. Initially, they may be guarded, but that's ok. You're going to circle back to this in subsequent meetings.

It's critical to understand each of your team member's hopes, dreams, and desires. Your job, as a locked on leader, is to facilitate their becoming self-actualized. Hopefully, that means being a part of your team, but their aspirations might be a better fit for another team. If so, you need to make it your mission to help them get on that team, regardless of where that team exists. If you already know what they want to accomplish, ask them about their progress towards their goals.

Ask how they are adjusting to the job, what challenges they have, and what you can do to help them. Finally, find out what they are enjoying the most. If they have done something noteworthy, compliment them on it and ask them how they did it or what their thought process was. Get them to brag. Not only will you gain insight into their mental processes, you will gain their trust. People like to be appreciated and they like to brag about their accomplishments. When you give them permission to do so, it improves their rapport with you.

Do not use these meetings to chastise, critique or otherwise hold someone accountable. If you do, they will start to shut down and you won't learn anything. You need to create an environment where it is safe for them to voice their opinion.

Finally, end on a high note. Start off each meeting by asking them about personal things which allows them to talk about themselves. End every meeting on positive accomplishments or what they enjoy. By doing so, your team members will feel relaxed and look forward to the meetings, making them more effective.

Frequency

For new team members these meetings should be more frequent than for established team members. I recommend once a week for the first month. If they are adjusting and performing, then you can stretch it out biweekly and then monthly. I'm not a fan of more frequent one-to-one meetings than once a month. They should be something team members look forward to. When I was growing up, there were occasions when I got to go to work with my dad, a high school music teacher. I'd hangout in his classroom and we'd go to lunch. They are some of my fondest memories of my dad because it was just him and me. Neither of my brothers were there (they had their own special times with him). You want your team to feel the same way about these meetings.

Recognition

Providing recognition for a job well done is probably the most obvious way to create esteem. Recognition can be either formal or informal. Formal recognition includes awards, plaques and commendations. In contrast, informal recognition comes in the form of an "'at a boy" or "job well done." On the surface, this seems like the easiest to accomplish. Yet, all too often I see it done so poorly that instead of building esteem and solidifying the team, it has the opposite effect.

Informal Recognition

Informal recognition can be done wrong. Imagine the following scenario: you are part of a team and work in an office with 10 other team members. Before you were hired, you went through a battery of interviews and assessments. The hiring manager spent a great deal of time getting to know you and what makes you tick. During this process, there were times that you weren't sure if you were going to make the cut. When you finally received an offer letter, it was an exciting and heady event. You celebrated with some close friends because you really thought this would be a great job. Then the company put you through some great training. The training was thorough and a little difficult. You notice a new hire in your class bailing out halfway through the training. You feel good, you know your job, what is expected of you, and how to effectively accomplish your tasks. The President of the company took you to lunch on your first day. When you pass him in the halls, he always greets you by name. You've learned that he sends out regular communications talking about the "company way" and how "we are different." He talks about your higher purpose and the good you are contributing to your community.

Your immediate manager seems like an OK sort. He greeted you warmly on your first day and seems likeable. He brought you to your cubicle and said, "Welcome to the gopher farm." You aren't 100% sure why they call the cubicles that but you've heard it before so, it doesn't take on any significance. At the end of your first day, your manager tells the entire team "good job" but you aren't sure why. You figure you'll learn as it's only your first day. You attack your work eagerly each day, but soon notice a pattern.

You aren't comfortable with how much time many of your coworkers spend on socializing. You notice their little heads popping up over the cubicle walls as they chat with neighbors. Then, it hits you. They look like the gophers in your yard sticking their heads out of their holes. Now you know why it's a gopher farm. Some team members are browsing the web or doing personal things while others aren't afraid of hard work, they're able to sleep right next to it.

However, you keep your nose to the grindstone. Your parents didn't raise any shirker. You've agreed to work for the company and work you will. Then, one day, the manager steps out of his office, or "ivory tower," situated right off the gopher farm. He has a big window so he can see what's going on, or at least he could if he didn't have his blinds down all day. When you first started, you noticed his door was usually closed. At first, you assumed he had important meetings or phone calls. Slowly, you realized his "open door" policy meant you had to open his door to speak with him. When you started and had to ask him a lot of questions, it didn't seem strange that he was always available, even when his door was closed. But now, you realize that the door wasn't closed because he was busy. Instead, he was isolating himself from his charge—the gopher farm.

Today, however, is different. First off, you are a little off your game. It has been a long week, and it's only Wednesday. You have a combination of some personal stuff going on and maybe your biorhythms are a little low. As a result, you're not as productive today as you've been in the past. You're still more productive than most of your coworkers, just not up to your own standards. Towards the end of the day, the boss emerges from his ivory tower. He casts his gaze around the room, then starts to walk up and down the aisles of cubicles, chatting briefly with a few people, as he meanders towards the exit door. Before leaving, he turns around and projects in a loud and authoritative voice, "Great job today, team! Keep up the good work. I really appreciate every-thing you are doing. I'll see you all tomorrow."

"What was that? Where did that come from?" you ask your-self. A buzz circulates around the room. You overhear one of the seasoned veterans of the team refer to the "leadership retreat" the manager had just attended. That makes sense; he probably learned he needed to show more appreciation to the employees for their hard work. The problem, you think to yourself, is that many people aren't working that hard. In fact, today was one of your least productive days, and the boss had no clue. You begin to think, "Maybe I've been pushing myself too hard. I don't have to work that hard to still be better than most everyone else." At this point, you figuratively put your hand on the throttles and pull them back at least partway. You realize you don't need to give 100% since it isn't recognized anyway.

You continue this way for a while, all the time, not feeling great about yourself. Then you make a decision and your Sunday routine changes. Now, instead of grabbing a cup of coffee and perusing the news and articles of interest, you look at job boards and help wanted ads on the internet. You reach out to recruiters and start looking for work. You conclude that you need to work hard, but you also need your hard work to be recognized and appreciated.

Finally, the day comes. You hand in your letter of resignation and provide a two-week notice to your boss. He asks you why and you explain you couldn't pass up an opportunity where you'd earn more money with a better title. You don't bother telling him you wouldn't have even looked for a new job if you felt more appreciated. You let him think it was the money because it's just easier.

This scene is not atypical. It happens in companies and organizations across the country and around the world thousands of times every day. Although well-intentioned, the boss's ineffective praise did more harm than good. I refer to this particular technique as "Carpet Bombing Praise." According to a study by hr.com and sponsored by Lifeworks,[24] 76% of employees who don't feel valued at work are seeking other job opportunities. The same study indicates that offering specific praise is associated with employees feeling valued and recognized.[25]

In the early days of air warfare, dropping bombs accurately was 80% luck and 20% skill. At the end of WWI, the U.S. Military recognized a need for a precision bombsight for bombing accurately from level flight. After six years of research, the Norden Bombsight was born. Since objects dropped from an airplane have the velocity of the airplane, bombs will continue moving forward as they fall. However, winds at altitude as well as drag from the air will slow the forward progress of the bomb while gravity speeds it up on its way down. The result is bombs fall along a curved path that is highly unpredictable. Although bombsights like the Norden made it easier to predict where the bomb will hit, they still were not that accurate by today's standard. During WWII, to qualify as a "Distinguished Bombardier," the highest rank attainable as a bombardier, you needed an average error of 172 feet. This is the very edge of the blast radius of a 500 lb. bomb. Actual accuracy under combat conditions was much less. The U.S. Army Air Corp (the pre-cursor to the Air Force) defined the target area as a circle with a 1,000 ft radius. Since the blast radius of a single, 500-lb. bomb is only 260 feet it would take four bombs, accurately dropped, to hit a target. In practice, this meant that to ensure the target was destroyed, they had to lay down a carpet of bombs, thus the term "carpet bombing." Unfortunately, this practice was hell on the non-military targets in the vicinity.

When the Allies wanted to destroy the industrial and communications complex in Dresden, Germany, they flew over 700 aircraft and deployed 3,900 tons of high explosive "dumb" bombs, carpeting the target area in ordinance. As a result, 25,000 civilians were killed creating a controversial public relations nightmare that persists today.

Now, we have more sophisticated methods of guiding bombs including laser guidance. A target is illuminated with a laser. The bomb has the ability to detect the reflected laser light and make corrections to its flight path to ensure a direct hit. As a result, laser-guided bombs hit a specific window in a building, not just the building. When we praise our team members for their accomplishments, our praise has to be as precise as a laser-guided weapon.

L.A.S.R.-Guided Praise

Providing LASR-guided praise is actually simple if you follow a few basic rules.

L = Limited to the individual or team that performed well

Limit your praise to the person or team that earned the praise. As we saw in our earlier scenario, the less specific you are about who did a good job, the less effective the praise, to the point where it becomes counterproductive. This means that you must be aware of what is going on within your organization. You have to stay connected by walking the floor and talking with your front-line supervisors. You don't need to be able to do the work, but you must know how it should be done. Otherwise, how will you know when it is done correctly? How will you know what is praiseworthy? By staying connected, you will find areas needing improvement or uncover potential problems before they arise or grow big.

A = About the company core values demonstrated

If you want to reinforce the importance of your company's values, give them a voice. Don't miss the opportunity to reinforce your organizational values. This shows everyone, not just the person receiving the praise, that your values are more than just words on a wall. When you praise a team member because they demonstrated one or more of your values, others will emulate the mindset.

S = Specific to the behavior you want to reinforce

In the late 19th century, Edward L. Thorndike conducted a series of experiments showing how behaviors are modified based on the consequences of those behaviors. He placed hungry cats in a puzzle box and watched them attempt to escape to get food. He observed that when a behavior is followed by a satisfying consequence, the behavior will be reinforced and repeated. When the consequence is unpleasant, the behavior is less likely to be repeated.

As a result, the cats got better, that is faster, at figuring out how to open the puzzle box on subsequent attempts. Thorndike's theory is known as the "Law of Effect" or "Operant Conditioning."

In the mid 1900's, psychologist B. F. Skinner extended the work of Thorndike to show that *all* behaviors are a result of operant conditioning. Skinner showed we don't need to wait until the behavior is perfect before we reinforce it. We can shape behavior by rewarding or reinforcing subsequent improvements in behavior. If you want a Customer Service Rep to show more empathy on the phone, reinforce a time when they showed empathy during a call. As the behavior improves, reinforce the improvements until eventually you get the behavior you want. Skinner further theorized that if the reinforcer is removed, the learned behavior will eventually become extinct. We need periodic performance reviews that reinforce the behaviors we need repeated.

Great, this means that people being rewarded are more likely to repeat the behavior, but what about everyone else? There is another theory in psychology called Observational Learning. According to Albert Bandura, Professor Emeritus at Stanford University, we can also learn by watching others.[26] Many factors influence whether or not we will learn from observation. By reinforcing observed behavior, you can enhance learning. When we identify the specific behavior a team member did well and reward it by complimenting them, everyone who observes the reward are more likely to "learn" from the event, and therefore replicate it. That's one of the reasons the old adage, "Praise in public, chastise in private" is so important. More on the chastising when we discuss accountability.

R = Real time, give praise as close to the event or behavior as possible

Laser-targeted specific praise should be timely and as close to the praiseworthy event as possible. If you did something noteworthy on Monday morning and I don't provide you praise until Friday, it will be less effective.

Let's look at how you might apply this. Take the example of a Customer Service Rep at a moving company who handles a difficult customer on the phone. Empathy is one of the company's core values and its mission to "eliminate the stress of moving." Laser-targeted praise might be, "You did a great job dealing with Mr. Jones on the telephone. I love the way you listened patiently while he vented, then validated his feelings before fixing the issue. You demonstrated empathy, one of our core values while reducing his stress. This is the whole reason we exist as a company, great job!" As you can see, this feedback targets specific behaviors that replicate and reinforce the company's values and mission.

Besides supervisory recognition, you can have peer recognition. There are several ways to do this effectively. One of the biggest trends is a "Good Book." These books can be physical or digital. Team members can make a note whenever another team member does something good. As part of the agenda, during weekly team meetings, the team leader reads the new entries for the week.

There are also many peer recognition platforms. Bonus.ly (https://bonus.ly) allows team members to receive recognition and recognize others. You can force them to state what organizational values and specific behavior took place. The recognition is distributed to the team and the recipient receives points. The amount of points is determined by whomever is recognizing the accomplishment. Points can be traded in for rewards. Typically, you can tailor your rewards catalog by team or location. If you are an international organization, the rewards can be different for each location, thereby ensuring the gifts are meaningful to the recipients. Many of these platforms let you to survey your employees to determine engagement, allowing you to tweak your program for maximum impact.

Formal Recognition

Formal recognition usually comes in the form of awards. For many companies, these are "Most Valuable Player/Person (MVP)," "employee of the month," "employee of the quarter," and/or "employee of the year" awards. However, you can be very creative here as you think about recognizing teams within your organization.

Just like with informal recognition, this is the time to drive home the importance of your values, mission, and higher purpose. You provide weight to them by memorializing these attributes with a formal award. Besides your values, you can also recognize milestones and accomplishments that support the importance of the metrics you put in place. Formal recognition should not be taken lightly. A great deal of thought should go into who and how they are recognized.

Apply LASR focus to your formal recognition program. The extent of the process should be proportional to the importance of the award. Much more time and energy should be devoted to the company's "Team Member of the Year Award" than a department's "Team Member of the Month."

Whenever possible, apply objective standards to the award criteria. Frequently it involves some subjectivity. According to his citation, Congressional Medal of Honor recipient Gunnery Sergeant John Basilone's actions during the Battle for Henderson Field demonstrate "gallantry and intrepidity at risk of life above and beyond the call of duty." The assertion that he demonstrated these traits may sound subjective. However, the indisputable facts are he ran 200 yards, between machine gun emplacements, while under direct enemy fire, to carry ammunition, countless times; was responsible for single-handedly killing 38 enemy combatants; he fought for 72 hours without rest and was one of three marines from his unit left alive at the end of the battle. When Gunnery

Sergeant Basilone received his Congressional Medal of Honor, there was no doubt that it was deserved. If you want to hold your awards in similar esteem, the worthiness of your recipients should be equally as obvious.

Establish a standing award process that, at a minimum, details who can nominate someone for the award, what documentation is required, and who is responsible for determining the recipient. For your higher awards, consider having a committee to minimize any perception of favoritism or subjectivity.

Medals, Ribbons and Campaign Badges

"You call these baubles, well, it is with baubles that men are led... Do you think that you would be able to make men fight by reasoning? Never. That is only good for the scholar in his study. The soldier needs glory, distinctions, and rewards." ~ Napoleon Bonaparte on Awards[27]

When you see a service member in uniform, your eye is immediately drawn to the myriad of decorations on one or both chests. To the civilian who has never served, you may not know what these ribbons mean, but they are impressive nonetheless. To another service member, these decorations tell a story. They represent both personal and unit accomplishments as well as where, when, and how someone served. Some may have derogatory nicknames, like the National Defense Service Medal, also known as the "I've got a pulse medal" since it was awarded to everyone serving during a specified time. Others like the Distinguished Flying Cross and the Bronze or Silver Star are highly honored because they represent gallant service. Still others, such as any of the Service Cross or our highest honor, the Congressional Medal of Honor, represent a level of gallantry and heroism that is legendary.

I remember being in Aviation Officer's Candidate School. As we marched around going from class to class, we were all acutely aware of the lack of ribbons on our uniforms. Our first chance to receive a ribbon was about halfway through training when we learned to fire a sidearm. We went out to the firing range and, under instruction from our Drill Instructor, Gunnery Sergeant Bernie Jones, USMC, we were instructed in the finer points of the care and handling of a .38 caliber revolver. We were all aware what we needed to score in order to receive the Marksman Medal. Additionally, if we wanted to adorn the medal with a Sharpshooter's -S- or Expert's -E- we knew those scores as well. Shortly thereafter, many of us were proudly sporting our first ribbons as they represented an accomplishment.

Ribbons and medals are earned, not won. It is common to hear civilians say someone "won" the Bronze Star or Distinguished Service Cross as if it is a contest. Whether it is the highest or lowest medal, each is earned. As Napoleon Bonaparte said to the captain of HMS Bellerophon on his way to exile,[28] "A soldier will fight long and hard for a piece of colored ribbon." Your troops will likewise strive for a similar tangible recognition. Let's look at how you might provide it.

How One Company Handles Recognition

Snacknation provides custom, healthier snack boxes to the home or office. When Chelsie Lee, Sr. Vice President, was hired, one of her responsibilities was to build and improve the performance of their "Member Success Team" (MST). At Snacknation, the MST is responsible for sales and retention of Snacknation's customers. Chelsie set out to build a subculture within Snacknation's larger culture. Snacknation's CEO was focused on holding the team accountable for hitting their numbers. He wanted Chelsie to point out to team members when they fell short of the metrics. Chelsie took a different approach. She designed a recognition program where team members earn badges for hitting milestones related to their most important metrics.

Chelsie asked Clay Telfer, a team member, to design a series of buttons. These are the kinds of buttons you pinned onto your denim when you were a kid (or at least I did). Each type of button has a different icon. They are awarded based on hitting milestones that are related to the metrics important to their group. For example, if your company provides remote computer support, a key metric might be the number of support tickets a technician closes on the first contact. You can have awards for achieving 100 first contact resolutions. In Snacknation's case they had awards for customer saves (keeping a customer that is trying to cancel), upsells, and average customer response time. As a result of this and other initiatives Chelsie implemented, her team is energized and engaged.

Snacknation allows their MST members to telecommute, however, team members typically prefer to work in the office unless they have a commitment like going to a doctor's appointment. There is a corresponding positive business result due to the culture of the MST. The number of accounts that cancel service has been reduced from about 7% to as low as 3%. Chelsie acknowledges many factors go into this reduction including improved product offerings. However, if the team isn't engaged, the company would not have known how to modify their products to appeal to more of their customers.

Because recognition is how you tell your team what behaviors you want more off, Chelsie was willing to create an elaborate way of recognizing her team. Most managers hold people accountable for errors. However, holding people accountable helps eliminate behaviors you don't want. By recognizing behaviors you want repeated, your team knows how to replace the bad behaviors with the good ones.

Chelsie recommends breaking your awards down into different groups.

The Girl Scout Badge: This badge represents milestones. In Naval aviation, you get a century patch to wear on your flight jacket for every 100 carrier landings on the same ship. The more century patches, the more experienced the pilot or naval flight officer. You can do something similar based on your metrics. In a customer service department responsible for customer retention, badges could be earned for the first, 25th, 100 th, etc. customer saved. A computer technician could earn contact resolution badges in a similar fashion. A salesperson could earn a badge for "$100,000 in revenue generated." The distinguishing character-istic of the Girl Scout Badge is everyone can earn these and they illustrate competence and, therefore, show how you hold people in esteem.

The Campaign Ribbon: In the military, we received these for campaigns in which we took part, such as the Afghanistan Campaign Medal or Vietnam Service Medal. In business, they can commemorate specific events like a product rollout, a conten-tious meeting, or maybe a crisis that was successfully navigated. These connote someone has experience in those "one off" situa-tions that are rare, but provide the experience needed to navigate the next "one off" situation that comes along.

The Stanley Cup: These are the awards that only one per-son holds at a time. Like the Stanley Cup, your name goes on it, but then it gets passed on to the next recipient. Examples may include: most sales in a month/quarter/year; most resolved ser-vice tickets; or most aging receivables collected.

The Evergreen: Like the Expert Pistol Medal, these rep-resent achieving specific skills. Chelsie recommends using these when on-boarding new employees. At the moving company, badges could be awarded after completing each level of training. What I love about this is at a glance you know who is qualified to do what and where a team member needs to focus their efforts to be better rounded.

To ensure that your awards are not capricious or politically motivated, create written, formal award criteria, a nomination process, and a committee to vet the award nominees and determine who has earned the awards. Include a ceremony to commemorate the awardee (a purpose-built tradition). Be careful here, not everyone is comfortable in the spotlight. For minor awards, consider simply reading names and not forcing people to come up and accept them in front of a large group. For more important awards, you might offer someone a chance to say a few words. Ask them first in private so they don't feel obligated. If they are uncomfortable with public speaking, then you don't want to embarrass them and have any negativity attached to the award.

Our primary goals with any recognition program are to make sure the recipient feels good about being recognized and they are recognized for something specific. This is not the time for "participation medals" that do nothing more than dilute the success of those who deserve recognition and bring down the morale of the team.

Delegation

Another, often overlooked, but powerful way to build esteem in individual team members is by delegating additional responsibility beyond what is in their job description. Like recognition, delegation can either bolster morale and a sense of esteem or, if done poorly, hurt esteem and ultimately the productivity of your team.

While I was deployed on the U.S.S. Nimitz (CV-69) with Fighter Squadron Two-Eleven, in the middle of the Pacific Ocean, I was asked to report to the CAG's office. The CAG is the Commander of the Air Wing, which is comprised of all of the squadrons deployed on the Aircraft Carrier. In other words, he is my boss's boss. I knew the CAG and he knew me since I frequently flew as his RIO when he flew with our squadron, but this was the first time I had been asked to report to his office. When I arrived, I was pleasantly surprised, and a little honored. He asked me to plan a force protection mission for an upcoming exercise.

This exercise was a little unusual because I had to develop a plan to defend the battle group from an unknown enemy who might attack from any direction. Typically, a carrier battle group has a known threat sector so it is only concerned with defending itself in a pre-defined direction. Missions like this are normally planned by the Air Wing staff and not an officer in one of the squadrons that make up the Air Wing. However, as a Lieutenant on my second deployment, the CAG wanted to give me an opportunity to expand my knowledge and gain some needed experience. One of the lessons the military learned thousands of years ago is that everyone needs to be prepared to do the job of their superiors. In battle, no one is immune from harm. To that end, we are constantly training our subordinates to take over our jobs. I find this approach lacking in the civilian world.

After my meeting with the CAG, I had a clear understanding of my mission objective, to coordinate the Air Wing's efforts with those of the cruisers and destroyers that made up our escort ships and prevent an incursion by hostile forces. What I didn't have, however, was any kind of operational plan. The problem was since I didn't know where the threat was coming from, an area we referred to as the "threat sector," I had to develop a plan to defend a circle that was 400 miles in diameter around the ship. That meant we had to protect over 1,256 square miles with the limited assets we had in the battle group.

Fortunately, a Lieutenant Commander from our E2 Hawkeye squadron approached me. They are the airborne early warning radar aircraft that are the eyes of the fleet. You've seen them, they're the aircraft with the giant Frisbee on their backs. If we had a limited threat sector, we would station an E2 a safe distance away from the ship in the direction of the threat. Since their radar can see farther than the 200 miles we needed to protect, we could react and get our fighters out there before the enemies entered their missile engagement range. Since we didn't have enough E2's to cover the airspace that needed to be protected, we had to have another plan. The E2 Lieutenant Commander wanted to test an idea.

I was relieved. With the skeleton of a plan, I went to work. I found myself immersed in a new world. During my first cruise, Iraq had invaded Kuwait and started Operation Desert Storm. At that time, my sole planning responsibility was to become the subject matter expert on the Iraqi air-to-air missile systems and brief my fellow aircrewmen on them. The planning of the war was left to the more experienced aircrew. Now it was my turn.

I had to figure out which aircraft we were going to have on the flight deck. It's not like the movies where you just bring new aircraft up from the hangar bay whenever you need to. Massive coordination is required. Then, I had to plan our ordinance load out and make sure the ship's Weapons Department had them in the bomb farm on the starboard side of the ship's island. Communications plan, launch sequence, refueling & recovery plans, contingency plans all had to be developed. In addition, I had to coordinate with the destroyers and cruisers so everyone knew who was responsible for which piece of the sky. The plans needed to ensure that our aircraft could safely traverse their airspace without being shot down. Each step of the way, I learned limitations that forced me to think three or four steps ahead. The internal operations of an aircraft carrier are deeply intermeshed and nothing is done in a vacuum.

My learning curve was steep but, through it, an entire new world opened up to me. Since I was developing a new plan never executed before, I was asking strangers in departments I had never interfaced with to do things they had not done before. At no time did anyone offer resistance. Instead, they provided me with feedback as to why things were difficult and suggestions on what needed to be changed to get them done. Everyone was focused on the mission like their lives depended on it, because it did. Although this was an exercise, we all knew that it could turn into a real-world operation overnight.

I developed the plan, frequently backtracking as I discovered some operational limitations to which I was newly privy. I periodically reported to the CAG and his Operations Officer. They would grill me on the details, asking hard but important questions. If I didn't have the answer I had to go and get it, then report back. Finally, I got the CAG's approval.

Then I created the briefings for all the units involved. I reviewed the mission with the four fighter squadrons, including my own, as well as the squadron that was providing the tanking support. Finally, it was execution day. After an Air Wing-wide briefing on the closed-circuit TV system, the crews had their individual briefs. I sat in Combat Operations and watched the mission unfold. My job was to advise the CAG if any adjustments needed to be made during the operation. Several hours later, we recovered our last aircraft. The mission was a success. The pride I felt was palpable. I had briefly transcended from a cog in the machine, someone who showed up and did what they were told, to something new. Although I had planned many squadron missions, planning and executing an operation for the entire Air Wing was a more complex challenge and proportionately more gratifying. My esteem increased and my value to the team amplified. The enjoyment for what I did was greater and I could now contribute more to the team. That is one of the most powerful effects when we delegate properly. Like every successful leadership tactic, we create a win-win scenario.

The Do's and Don'ts of Delegating

Before we get into how to effectively delegate, we need to understand what delegating isn't. It's not a way for you to avoid doing your job or to foist your responsibilities onto a subordinate. Permanently delegating one of your duties onto a team member without some kind of compensation will have a deleterious effect on them.

There are two primary reasons we should delegate a task:

1. **Free our time so we can do something more important.** By the way, lowering your golf handicap is not more important. If you are given a more strategic project that takes your time, then delegating an important but less critical responsibility makes sense. Both tasks or projects need to get done. Since you don't have time to get them both done within the time requirement, enlist help from a team member.

2. **Team member development.** The military is constantly training for battle and in battle, everyone is vulnerable. This means you need to be able to fill in for the person above you in the chain of command. If the Company Commander is killed or incapacitated, his XO takes over. Then the next senior officer becomes the XO and everyone moves up accordingly. If a Fire Team Leader is incapacitated the Assistant Fire Team Leader moves up, etc. Even in peace time, you either move up or move out. There is a constant flow of new blood. Company grade officers become field grade officers, and then become flag officers. Each step of the way the cadre is winnowed down. If you don't make the cut, you are released and make room for the next cohort of officers. There is a similar movement in the enlisted ranks to senior noncommissioned officers.

In civilian companies and organizations there is similar movement. However, the exception is you can become stuck at a level and never promoted or let go. Regardless, we should always be grooming our replacement. The test of whether or not a particular tactic is a good leadership tactic is determining if it is a true triple-win. Training your team members as your replacement absolutely passes this test. Let's examine how.

First, the team member wins. When we delegate, in effect, we teach a team member new skills. They learn to work above their paygrade and, therefore, become more valuable to the organization. The more we increase a team member's value, the more:

- esteem they gain from our tribe,
- secure they become in the organization or business, and
- compensation or promotions they can earn.

As you can see, the team member definitely wins when you delegate.

You win when you delegate, too. Delegation is like cloning yourself. When you have a team member take on a task or project you would otherwise do yourself it allows you to more effectively multitask. It also provides an opportunity to evaluate a team member on their strengths and weaknesses. You can uncover areas that need development or refinement. When done right, you do this without putting the organization or team member at risk for failure. You become a more effective leader as well because you are able to objectively gauge team member development, pinpoint areas of strength that you can leverage, and areas of weakness that need to be reinforced or somehow mitigated. In short, your productivity will increase and this will be noticed by your reporting seniors. As your department's productivity increases, your worth to the organization increases, too. You definitely win.

Your organization wins from having a cadre of individuals who are groomed for advancement. As companies grow, they need more talented leaders and managers. If you have a team member that is ready to step into your role, then you are available to move up as well. Everyone wins when a company promotes from within. The organization gains senior teammates that understand and thrive in the culture ensuring the company's identity remains consistent. By breeding more, like-minded individuals who share the values that drive the organization it reinforces the sense of safety and security you created when you defined a clear career path. It shows your company has integrity.

Be on Mission

In my years of experience, people generally make one of two mistakes when they delegate. First, they don't provide enough information and then flip out when they get results that don't come close to what they needed or expected. Second, they tell the team member exactly how to do the task or project, as if they are doing it themselves. Since communication is never 100% accurate, it takes longer for the project to be completed and the person becomes nothing more than a remote control. When CAG assigned me the task of planning the exercise, he did neither of the two. He approached the problem of delegation the same way we approached planning any mission.

If we were planning a strike on an enemy command and control bunker, we had to first define our mission objective. Is it to destroy the bunker, disrupt their operations or destroy their command and control capabilities? We looked at the available resources such as aircraft that could jam the enemy's radars or a fighter escort to keep the enemy's aircraft off us. We asked, "What kind of ordinance did we have available and how would it affect our target?" The next step was deciding when this had to happen—literally down to the last second. We planned our ingress and egress routes with intermediate checkpoints so we knew where and when we had to be there in order to make our 10-second target window. Then, we discussed what could go wrong and finally, how we'd adapt and adjust if and when things did go wrong. We did one final review, a mission briefing, to make sure nothing was missed and that everyone knew their jobs. Finally, we debriefed every mission determining what went right, what could have gone better, and what we could learn from it.

To remember how to delegate, I like the acronym **M.I.S.S.I.O.N.**, which stands for:

Mission objectives: make sure you know what success looks like. In my case, my objectives were: (1) make sure that no aircraft entered within the missile launch zone without being visually determined to not be armed, and (2) make sure no aircraft flew over the battle group without a fighter escort.

Include resources that are available: Make sure you provide sufficient resources to your delegate. The CAG gave me access to departments and personnel with whom I didn't normally work.

Suggest **S**paringly: Ask questions rather than make suggestions. Word your question to show how you think about a problem. Instead of giving specific directions, ask questions that point out potential pitfalls like, "What are the possible negative consequences?" Only give specific direction when absolutely necessary as you are trying to develop a mindset and skill, not create a voice-activated robot.

Intermediate check points: Check on the progress at sufficient intervals to make corrections if needed. You don't want to do the work, but you need to make sure the task doesn't go off track. The frequency will vary based on the team member's experience level, the complexity of the assignment, and timeline for completion. Since you have experience doing the assignment, you decide.

One final review: Review a final time before executing.

a**N**alyze the results: After implementation, debrief about the process and the initiative. This is your chance to determine if they actually understood all the lessons.

As you start delegating effectively, you will find your team is more productive and more inspired. You will easily identify your rising stars and know where their strengths lie and where they need to develop. So, stay on M.I.S.S.I.O.N.!

Accountability

"It is not enough that we do our best, sometimes you have to do what is required."

-WINSTON CHURCHILL

It's January of 1987. I walk down the portable staircase from the airplane onto the ramp at Pensacola International Airport. At the tender young age of 25, I had just completed my first ever jet flight. I flew from Philadelphia, where I was born and raised, to Pensacola, Florida. I was to report to my first duty station for the U.S. Navy, Aviation Officer Candidate's School located at Naval Air Station Pensacola. The hour is late, after 10 pm or 2200 hours as I was to learn. It is threatening rain. Growing up in Philadelphia, I thought I knew rain, but I came to realize that I knew as much about rain as I knew about the U.S. Navy. I was about to learn a great deal about both of these.

As I am making my way to the taxi queue outside the terminal, another man approaches me. He is going to NAS Pensacola and wants to share a cab. It turns out he is another officer candidate. My orders are to report to the "quarter deck for NAVAVSCOLSCOM," whatever that is. Our cab stops at the front gate, where the sentry checks our orders, then directs the cab driver to the building that houses Naval Aviation Schools Command (ahh, NAVAVSCOLSCOM revealed!), the command responsible for Aviation Officer Candidate School or AOCS. Wow, the Navy sure loves its acronyms.

After our orders are stamped, indicating our arrival, we are directed to go to regimental headquarters, diagonally across the street. I step out onto the porch and gaze out at what I hope to be my final destination for the night. Through the squall that had opened up while I was inside, I see a brick and plaster antebellum building, replete with colonnades capped with plinths in the Greek style. The rain stops as suddenly as it came on, so we dash across the street. As we approach, I notice two other young men, one in civilian clothes, like me, and the other in a white uniform. The civilian is standing in a position approximating that of attention, back against the brick wall of the building, hands at their sides. From halfway across the street I can hear the guy in white screaming at the top of his lungs, "Don't you eyeball me! Pick a spot 1,000 yards away and look at that! Heels together, feet at a 45-degree angle, head up, chest out, hands on the seams of your trousers!" Clearly, the civilian had never been in the Boy Scouts or marching band.

I am about to learn that the guy in white is a candidate officer. Fourteen weeks before this, he was just like me, confused and apprehensive as he joined his class for the first time. Now, along with the rest of his surviving class of candidates, he is administratively running the two training battalions and the regimental headquarters as a candidate officer. He will be graduating at the end of the week and will receive his commission as an Ensign in the United States Navy. Of course, I don't know any of this as I run up the main steps of the building into a maelstrom of noise and confusion like I had never seen before, nor since.

As I reach the veranda, I spy, to the side of the foyer just inside, a Dutch door with the bottom half closed. On the top of the bottom section of door is a ledge and on the ledge is a ledger. Behind the door is another young man in white. He is yelling at the civilian who recently vacated the veranda where I now stood. The man behind the door is yelling something at the other civilian while he is trying to sign the ledger. All of this I notice in an instant. I come to a position of attention after I drop my trash— the single suitcase with the required five days worth of clothes and toiletries. I don't get much correction. I guess four years in marching band and time as a Boy Scout account for something. The candidate officer instructs me to look at his collar. He informs me that I am a "candidate" and that I can tell candidates because they will have a "fouled anchor" insignia on their collars. He then points out his insignia, two parallel gold bars. He then informs me, at the top of his lungs, that anyone with gold bars on their collars are candidate officers and will be addressed as sir or ma'am. I am then instructed to go inside and wait in a small line across from the Dutch door I had spied earlier.

Once inside, I take a moment. All around me, there are people in white yelling at people in civilian clothes. Civilians are running with candidate officers in hot pursuit, motivating them to greater speed. In spite of the seeming chaos all around me, I am in the eye of the storm as I await my turn at the Dutch door. I use the opportunity to surreptitiously observe my surroundings. I pay particular interest to the action at the Dutch door across the foyer from where I stand. The guardian of the book, as I've come to think of him, is bellowing at the civilian in front of the door. He yells, "Candidate, do not do anything until I have given you all the instructions. On the next line on the ledger I want you to legibly print your name, hometown and then sign your name in the space indicated without setting your hand down or touching the book. Does the candidate understand?" The civilian in front of the door yells back, "Yes sir!" The guy in white seems a little agitated and bellows back, "Candidate, this candidate is a candidate, does the candidate understand?" Again, the civilian replies, "Yes, sir." Turning a little redder, the guy in white repeats himself. Clearly, the civilian does not understand because, once again he shouts his reply, "Yes sir!" Nearly apoplectic, the guy in white spews out, along with some spittle, "No, candidate this candidate is a candidate! Does the candidate understand!" He did this while holding onto his left collar and pushing the insignia in my soon-to-be-classmate's face. Ahh, I get it. I now know what the candidate officer outside was trying to tell me.

Then, it's my turn. I am summoned to the Dutch door. The guy in white, although standing on the other side of the door, less than two feet away, barks at me in a voice they can hear back in Philadelphia. "Candidate, do not do anything until I have given you all the instructions. On the next line on the ledger I want you to legibly print your name, home town and then sign your name in the space indicated without setting your hand down or touching the book. Does the candidate understand?" he asked. I replied, "Yes candidate!" I watch him open his mouth to bellow his response when I see his brain catch up with his ears. The corners of his mouth turn up, ever so slightly. "Proceed" he replies and I carefully print my name, home of record, and sign, all without resting my hand on the book. Tired, anxious, and brimming with nervous energy, I doubt that the greatest forensic document examiner in the world could have attributed that scrawl to me. The candidate behind the door now completes the ritual, "You are now a member of the United States Navy and subject to the Uniform Code of Military Justice. Grab your trash and proceed up the stairs on your left. A Candidate Officer will direct you to your room, candidate!"

Little did I realize that as I climbed the stairs, that I was ascending into a new realm. The realm of absolute accountability. Over the next 14 weeks I would be inculcated into this realm and its culture of accountability. My locker was to be immaculate and organized identically to those of my classmates with everything folded just so. Our standard issue tighty whitey briefs were to folded into 4" x 4" squares, each identical. Within five minutes of reveille at 0430, our beds (we called them racks) had to be perfectly made, with hospital corners, tight as a drumhead and the top sheet folded down exactly 4" over the cover. Our Drill Instructors (Never ever call them a D. I.) would take one of our briefs and lay them on the turn down and they'd better be identical. Our uniforms had to be perfect, every piece of brass polished to a shine, in its proper place. Buttons buttoned, boots polished to a mirror-like shine, even after marching through mud or dirt. We were not allowed to use the first person. The word "I" was replaced by the phrase "this candidate." When talking to the Drill Instructor we were to sound off in a loud and forceful voice that had to cause the fire bell, mounted just below the ceiling in every hallway, to vibrate and ring. If one of us failed to do any of these things, we would all pay the price. When a mistake was made, the punishment was physical training, or P.T., as it was called.

Once, while standing in line for chow (a meal) there was a candidate from a class junior to mine in front of me. I didn't know him as he was from the other training battalion. The Chief Drill Instructor was in the Chow Hall and walking down the line of candidates waiting to eat. He asked the candidate in front of me why he was late for chow. The young and relatively inexperienced candidate replied, "Sir, the class was with our D.I." The Chief Drill Instructor went ballistic, "D.I.? D.I.? What is D.I? Damn Iranian? Drunk Irishman?" He went on forever with more possible terms for D.I. than I could ever imagine, much less remember. Then like a missile in terminal guidance, he honed in on the candidate's brass, the fouled anchor insignia we all wore on the collars of our khakis. The fouled anchor is an anchor that has a line attached to the ring at the top, loops over the stock, wraps around the shaft, and loops below the arm with the end of the rope, known as the "bitter end" off to one side. The bitter end is supposed to be pointing outboard, or away, from the head. The candidate had his brass on backwards.

By this time there was a huge gap in the chow line while the Chief Drill Instructor was berating the young candidate. I could have gone around with a simple "by your leave" but opted not to call attention to myself. Instead, I elected to hold my place until the Chief Drill Instructor was done with his victim. My mistake.

All of a sudden, the Chief Drill Instructor turned his sites on me, "Candidate, what is your name?" he snarled as he turned his gaze on me. "Sir, Aviation Candidate Rosenberg, class 13-87," I replied realizing that I was just caught in the switches. "And why, Candidate Rosenberg, did you not inform your shipmate that he had his collar brass on backwards?" he asked in a feral snarl. Before I had a chance to reply, he continued, "The two of you report to my office at 1800!" With that, he turned down the line, looking for his next target.

Accountability is a tool, one that is used well by the military. With it, we are taught to be responsible for ourselves, our team-mates, and our mission. Without accountability, people may try their best and fail, but when held accountable, they will do what is required.

Of the three critical tactics required to develop esteem, holding yourself and your team accountable is the most critical. There are two major reasons why your other efforts will be unsuccessful unless you achieve this objective.

1. **Damaged credibility.** Failure to hold your team account-able negatively impacts your credibility. If you don't call someone to task when a team member fails to execute, you are sending the message that you don't really mean what you say. This directly degrades your integrity. Your actions are not consistent with your words. As discussed in the first chapter, integrity is one of the three essential qualities of a leader. This doesn't mean you have to scream and yell, it doesn't mean you have to "punish," it simply means that they need to hold them accountable. We'll talk about how to do that shortly.

2. **Sending the wrong message.** Failure to hold a team member accountable tells them they aren't worth it. Let's face it, if we ask someone to do something they aren't capable of doing, and they don't succeed, we don't take them to task. If the task they failed at is a normal job duty, then we're actually saying, "You

aren't capable of doing your job." Since our membership is predicated on our contribution to the group, when we fail to hold a team member accountable, we are indicating their position in the group is at risk. When they lose their sense of safety and security, their ability to meet their physiological needs are at risk because they may not have a job.

Because you failed to hold that person accountable, the security blanket you created when you carefully selected your team, defined their duties, provided metrics for them, trained them, created a career path for them, and then developed the sense of community and culture that nourished them, unravels like pulling on a thread in a sweater.

The problem is compounded by observational learning. Behavior has to be reinforced for observational learning to take place. You can reinforce behavior through both positive reinforcement and negative reinforcement. When you provide something good or pleasant in response to a behavior, that's positive reinforcement. Contrary to popular belief, proving something unpleasant is not negative reinforcement. Negative reinforcement happens when you remove something unpleasant. If you expect to be held to answer for failing to accomplish a goal or task, typically an unpleasant event, you undergo stress, an unpleasant experience. If, however, the negative feedback is not forthcoming, then the stress is removed. The removal of stress is negative reinforcement. Those observing this are then likely to emulate the failure because it was reinforced.

Accountability Meetings

Failing to hold your team accountable can have a disastrous effect. Likewise, improperly holding someone responsible can have similar results. I have seen screamers, name callers, belittlers, and the like over the years. These would-be leaders blame their team for their ineffectiveness, never once realizing that the blame for the continued failures can be found in their mirrors.

Over the years, I've discovered that I need two different kinds of accountability meetings which are the Q-Board and the Counseling Session.

The Q-Board

My time in the military brought the inspiration of the Q-Board, or quality board. Whenever there is an aviation accident, a mishap board convenes. The purpose of this board is not to assign blame. Nothing discovered during this investigation can result in any kind of punitive action. The board's purpose is to discover the cause of the accident and then determine if any action is required to prevent its repeat.

Q-Boards are held whenever there is a service failure. Maybe it's a failure on the manufacturing line, a customer service issue, or personnel issue. I first used this process while running Priority Moving when I instituted the policy of issuing refunds for service failure, without argument, at the request of a customer. Therefore, I wanted to make sure we didn't repeat our mistakes. I wanted to make sure our policies and procedures weren't setting our crews up for failure. When we initiated the Q-Board process, we had well-documented procedures.

Every time a service failure occurred that either required us to refund money or I simply felt the service failure was egregious enough to warrant a board, we would convene. Our board consisted of me, as President, our VP of Operations, and our Warehouse Manager who was a very experienced mover and had been with us for some time. Our goal, as a board, was to make one of two determinations.

1. **Determine whether the service failure was systemic.** We wanted to know, "Did a policy or procedure cause the

error?" For example, a customer complained that six hours was too long to move out of a one bedroom apartment. The Q-board determined that our truck had to park a long distance away from the building (it was a large complex) and that meant it took a long time to walk from the apartment to the truck and back. Since we were familiar with the complex, we should have told the customer that this would take longer than a normal small move. We instituted a program that identified all of the complexes where similar conditions existed and then had our move coordinators set expectations with the customer. We further reinforced this by having our lead mover go over the expectations a second time at the start of the move.

By creating a process that allowed us to learn from our mistakes we created an environment that allowed us to constantly improve our services, create raving fans out of customers, and reduce the amount of money we needed to refund.

2. **Determine whether the service failure was a personnel issue.** We wanted to know, "Did a member of the crew ignore or contravene a procedure or policy for no good reason?" A lead mover decided to stop at a convenience store on the way to a customer's to start loading the truck. This caused the crew to be late, which meant they lost a convenient parking spot the client was trying to save for them, resulting in a long carry. The customer complained the move took too long and they received a partial refund. Our policy was to go directly from the warehouse to the client's without stopping en route. We provided water on every truck and crews were instructed that they had to bring any food, snacks, or additional fluids they might want to the warehouse because they couldn't stop. Once it was determined that the service failure was caused by a personnel issue, we had to decide whether additional training was required or more punitive action.

Organizing a Q-Board

When convening a Q-Board, it is critical that the subjects are not told the specifics of the service failure or complaint. Take the crew through all the procedures that started the evolution. In this case, we go through the entire move, step-by-step, procedure-by-procedure. Frequently, we uncover issues that, by themselves, would not have caused a Q-Board but it allowed us to reinforce training or modify policies.

The Q-Board removes the subjectivity associated with assessing someone's decision-making ability. We had one Lead Mover that was involved in three different Q-Boards. Although the only common denominator was the Lead Mover, that alone was significant. He was a likeable man, always with a smile, and no one had a bad thing to say about him. Yet, in spite of his training, he kept making costly mistakes. We concluded that this man's future was with another company. Our quality improved and we may not have recognized the pattern without the process.

Regardless of whether or not your procedures were as complete as ours, you should institute a Q-Board or similar procedure. As you conduct the boards, you will be forced to create effective policies and train to them.

The Counseling Session

Use Counseling Sessions when there is clearly some kind of personal behavior or performance issue and you plan on keeping the person. In the session, you will share that their performance or behavior is unacceptable and reveal what the consequences of not changing or improving will be. If the behavior rises to the level where immediate termination is called for then terminate the employee making sure to comply with your state's employment laws. For example, I had a mover put another mover into a "sleeper hold" until he passed out. This was a clear assault (well, technically battery). Although the assailant claimed he was just joking and the victim was in on it, it was clearly inappropriate. We suggested the victim file a police report, but he declined. In accordance with California law, I had HR issue a final check and terminated the assailant; there was no need for a Counseling Session.

In a Counseling Session, follow these rules:

1. **Come from a place of caring.** I put this first because it must be first in your heart and your head. Counseling sessions are about building people up, not tearing them down. Dr. Steven Covey is credited with saying, "start with the end in mind." The idea is to have a high-functioning team member. You don't do that by tearing people down. In order to do this, you need to have a high emotional IQ, or EQ. You have to be aware of your moods and emotions. If necessary, put them in a box and set them aside. If you have done everything right up to this point, I promise you that their failure is not personal. In fact, their failure is probably in equal parts your own.

2. **Always do it in private.** I can't emphasize this enough. If you want someone to be an effective part of your team, you need to maintain their dignity. If this is a team debrief, only the team should be part of it, never outside observers. You don't want people to become defensive or they won't absorb your input.

3. **Only discuss behaviors, never attitudes.** You may think they have a bad attitude but you don't really know what is going on in their head. When my employee, Rock from the moving company, came into our staff meeting, I thought he had a bad attitude. I was wrong, it turned out he was distracted by his daughter's illness. I have no doubt that if I had started my conversation with "Rock, your attitude sucks, what's going on?" I would have lost him. Behaviors are things we see, hear, and smell. Someone not smiling, arguing with a client, or yelling at a coworker is a

behavior. When we criticize attitudes, we open ourselves up for an argument. However, when we criticize behaviors that we observe, it is difficult to argue.

4. **Be specific.** The more generalized the criticism is, the less effective it is. Where applicable, provide metrics. The more objective you are, the less room for ambiguity and interpretation. This is also not the time for compliments.

5. **Separate your praise or recognition from holding someone accountable.** In other words, avoid the "compliment sandwich," the practice of opening with a compliment, giving the negative feedback, then closing with another compliment. This practice dilutes both your praise and your critique and makes you seem insincere. If you have created an open and candid culture, your feedback won't need the buttering up of the "compliment sandwich."

6. **Provide them with help.** Let them know what resources they have available to help them now and in the future. This can be personnel that are available to provide help, training resources, or reference resources. Anything you can think of that will help.

7. **Provide a time frame for performance improvement.** Make sure the time frame is realistic. Will they need to learn a new skill or improve a difficult skill? What's a reasonable time frame? This shouldn't be too long. If the realistic time frame is six months or more, consider intermediate improvement check points that build to the ultimate goal.

8. **Check in once a week to make sure they are on track.** This will show that you care and also let them know that this is serious. If something unexpected comes up, you'll be in front of it and able to deal with it before it gets out of hand.

9. **Be crystal clear about the consequences if they fail to improve or change their behavior.** This is not the time for ambiguities or colloquialisms, be direct and clear. You are not going to "give them a chance to expand their career horizons," you are "going to terminate them."

Create a counseling form. In the military, a page 13 entry into a member's personnel jacket is the counseling form. The counseling form should document the five critical elements:

1. Where they are deficient,
2. The changes that need to take place,
3. The time frame for change,
4. The resources available,
5. The consequences if the behavior isn't corrected.

Prepare the form ahead of time, then review it with the team member and ask them to sign it, acknowledging the conversation. If they don't want to sign it, then note that they wouldn't sign on their signature line with the time and date, then sign it yourself.

If done correctly, then one out of three team members will improve to an acceptable level of performance; another one out of three will recognize they aren't going to improve and will quit before any action is required on your part; another one out of three will need further discipline. If you have told them what they needed to do, provided the resources to do it, and sufficient time and they still failed to improve, you probably made a bad hire. Furthermore, they are probably not happy where they are any more than you are having them there. By telling them what they needed to do to avoid termination and they didn't improve, are you really firing them? In actuality, they did quit and they just lack the courage to do it, so they are making you do it.

Irrespective of how quickly I terminate an underperformer, the response from the rest of the team has been the same, "What took you so long?" So, don't feel bad, this too is a triple-win. The team wins because a weak performer is gone. You win because your team is now stronger. The former teammate wins because they now have the opportunity to find someplace where they will thrive.

CHAPTER 10

Thank G It's Monday!

*"If your actions inspire others to dream more, learn more,
do more and become more, you are a leader."*

~ John Quincy Adams

L eadership is about empowering people to do what they are meant to do. It's not rousing speeches that get the blood pumping, although that may be a tactic you employ. It's not yelling at your team to do better or berating them when they fall short. It's about setting people up for success, creating the conditions whereby they want to thrive. To do this successfully we have to leverage our inherent need for self-preservation. The formula for this was memorialized by Abraham Maslow in his Hierarchy of Needs. We know the formula works because 10,000 years ago, using these same principles, civilization was born.

Building a team is like building any project, it starts with the preparation. In our case, this means fulfilling the needs in Maslow's first two levels, our physiological needs and our safety and security needs. You meet the lowest level of physiological needs when you hire someone. However, that doesn't mean hire just anyone. Make sure you bring on team members that share your values and a passion for your higher purpose.

Maslow's second level of Safety and Security is handled when you create your Safety and Security Flight Plan. Establish a culture of corporate growth, create good job descriptions with simple metrics. Then train your team so they can do their job well and finally, create defined career paths that allow your team members to grow.

Once your preparation is complete, you move into the execution phase. Your hard work starts to pay off as you leverage your higher purpose and create esprit de corps. If your training is meaningful and rigorous, this should already be happening. Simultaneously, craft your purpose-built culture. This includes: your social organization, idioms that you use daily, your higher purpose, governance structure, and method of compensation. You'll want to make sure your customs and traditions are all in alignment with your values, reinforce those values, and celebrate those values.

Finally, hold your team in high esteem by recognizing their accomplishments, delegating greater responsibility, and holding them accountable when they fall short. Let them know their efforts matter to the outcome and their contribution is important. When you do all this, you open the door to self-actualization. The reality is you will lose some along the way, but know they will be happier elsewhere. Rejoice in their future success. Their replacement will be an upgrade, guaranteed.

In 1999, when I became the VP of Operations for a telecommunications company in San Diego, I had not fully developed my philosophy of being a locked on leader. I inherited 10 field technicians, one of whom, Randy, had the nominal title of "Supervisor." The owner told me he was worthless and they wanted me to let him go. I decided to see for myself before making any decisions. I started off by updating his job description as well as for the other technicians. I wanted them to know my expectations and memorialize it so there was no ambiguity. We had three levels of technicians, each with more responsibilities and requiring a greater skill set, culminating in the "field technician supervisor" position. I made the other techs answerable to him. In effect, I delegated authority to him that was nominally mine. I then started working with him so he understood that his job was to set our techs up for success. I had him create a training syllabus so the techs could become more competent and well-rounded. At the time, I only had three technicians that were completely competent to program the phone systems we serviced, three more that were competent at the basic programming, and four technicians that were only good for installing cabling and real basic work. Randy came alive as he was ceded more authority. He stepped up and became an excellent supervisor.

While we ended up losing four of the six technicians because we held them accountable, it was because of Randy that we didn't miss a beat. He made sure the remaining technicians all were the best they could be. After I left this position, Randy moved on to become the Operations Manager of a competitor until I lured him away and made him a business partner and Operations Manager of our own company a few years later. This was only possible because I used the tactics described in this book. Randy went from being dissatisfied to looking forward to work. After I left the company, he had to find another opportunity because he wasn't going to go back to the way it was, that is until I had something for him again.

That's the final gift of these tactics. When you implement them, you will find that you develop some deep and meaningful relationships with your team. Like the salty Chief Petty Officer who follows his Skipper from command to command, you will develop a cadre of elite individuals that will be as devoted to you and your mission as you are to them. They will follow you anywhere.

I've done these tactics for over 30 years and it has always been successful. I now speak on tactical leadership, give workshops, and coach my clients on how to successfully implement these programs. If you do this right, one day, you'll be walking down the hall and overhear someone say, "Thank g-d it's Monday and I'm back where I belong!" Then you will know the joy of enriching someone's life.

If you wish to book Dave to speak, schedule training, or learn more about how you can improve your team visit:

https://lockedonleadership.com
or email: info@lockedonleadership.com

Notes

1. Burkus, David, The Journal of Values Based Leadership, Vol 4, Issue 1, Winter/Spring 2011 > A Tale of Two Cultures: Why Culture Trumps Core Values in Building Ethical Organizations.
2. Johnson, Carrie (October 24, 2006). "Skilling Gets 24 Years for Fraud at Enron." The Washington Post.
3. Congressional Medal of Honor Citation for M/Sgt Vito Bertoldo.
4. David A. Garvin Alison Berkley Wagon Feld Liz Kind, "Google's Project Oxygen: Do Managers Matter?," Harvard Business Review, Rev July 29, 2013, p. 5.
5. "State of the American Workplace," Gallup Inc., p. 68.
6. John E. Hunter and Ronda F. Hunter, "Validity and Utility of Alternative Predictors of Job Performance," Psychological Bulletin, Vol 96, No. 1, 1984 p. 90.
7. Bill J. Bonnstetter and Judy I. Suiter, "The Universal Language DISC Reference Manual," Target Training International, Ltd., p. 32.
8. Ibid, p. 36.
9. TTI Success Insights, "Are You Ready to Train in the Fast Lane?." 2014, TTI Success Insights, p. 3.
10. David Sirota, Louis a. Mischkind and Michael Irwin Meltzer, "The Enthusiastic Employee,". Wharton School Publishing, 2005, p. 9.
11. Ibid p. 10.
12. Ibid p. 11.
13. Stephen M. Barbouletos, "The Impacts Of Discrepancy Between Role Expectations And Job Descriptions," University of Washington, 2011, p. 1.
14. Ibid p. 26.

15. Roman J, Older H, Jones WL. "Flight research program: VII. Medical monitoring of Navy carrier pilots In combat," Aerospace Med. 1967; 38:133-9.

16. Stan Phelps, "Five Customer-Centric Marketing Lessons from Apple to Zappos," forbes.com, August 18, 2014.

17. Abraham Maslow, "A Theory on Human Motivation," reproduced in Classics in the History of Psychology, Christopher D. Green, York University, p. 4.

18. Navern Pillay, Quraisha Dawood, Dr. Anis Mahomed Karodia, "The Relationship Between Career Development & Staff Motivation In The South African Petroleum Sector: A Case Study Of A Durban Refinery," Arabian Journal of Business and Management Review (Nigerian Chapter) Vol. 3, No. 2, 2015, p 47.

19. Ibid, p. 46.

20. Muzafer Sherif et al, The Robbers Cave Experiment, 1954, p. 1.

21. Ibid.

22. Bastian, Brock & Jetten, Jolanda & Ferris, Laura. (2014). Pain as Social Glue. Psychological science. 25. 10.1177/0956797614545886.

23. Chris Fussell, CW Goodyear, "One Mission: How Leaders Build a Team of Teams," Audible, 2017, Ch. 2, 00:01:33

24. Taking Care, How to Develop and Support Today's Employees, HR.com, 2017, p. 16

25. Ibid.

26. How Observational Behavior Affects Learning, Kendra Cherry, verywellmind.com, November 30, 2018.

27. On awards, as quoted in Mémoires sur le Consulat. 1799 à 1804 (1827) by Antoine-Claire, Comte Thibaudeau. Chez Ponthieu, pp. 83–84.

28. http://www.military-quotes.com/Napoleon.htm.dave

Made in the USA
Columbia, SC
17 March 2023